D0360972

JEREMIA
BIBLE STUDY SERIES

ROMANS

THE GOSPEL OF GRACE

DR. DAVID JEREMIAH

Prepared by Peachtree Publishing Services

THOMAS NELSON
Since 1798

Romans
Jeremiah Bible Study Series

© 2020 by Dr. David Jeremiah

All rights reserved. No portion of this book may be reproduced, stored in a retrieval system, or transmitted in any form or by any means—electronic, mechanical, photocopy, recording, scanning, or other—except for brief quotations in critical reviews or articles, without the prior written permission of the publisher.

Published in Nashville, Tennessee, by Thomas Nelson. Thomas Nelson is a registered trademark of HarperCollins Christian Publishing, Inc.

Produced with assistance of Peachtree Publishing Service (www.PeachtreePublishingServices.com). Project staff include Christopher D. Hudson, Randy Southern, and Peter Blankenship.

All Scripture quotations are taken from The Holy Bible, New King James Version. Copyright © 1979, 1980, 1982 by Thomas Nelson. All rights reserved.

Thomas Nelson titles may be purchased in bulk for educational, business, fundraising, or sales promotional use. For information, please e-mail SpecialMarkets@ThomasNelson.com.

ISBN 978-0-310-09162-2

Fourth Printing January 2021 / Printed in the United States of America

CONTENTS

INTRODUCTION TO
The Letter to the Romans

"For all have sinned and fall short of the glory of God" (Romans 3:23). With these words, the apostle Paul explains the basic problem all human beings share . . . and how we must all face the consequences for our sins (see 6:23). However, as Paul goes on to describe in his letter to the Romans, the good news is that God loves us in spite of our sin (see 5:8) and offers us a clear-cut path on how to receive His forgiveness and experience His salvation (see 10:9–10). Paul's letter to the Romans is simple in its explanation of the gospel, yet complex enough to challenge the hearts and minds of some of the greatest thinkers in Christian history, including Augustine, Martin Luther, and John Wesley. Paul explores the complexities that form the foundation of our "simple faith," contrasts justification by grace and justification by law, and even describes his own struggle to live a sanctified life. Through it all, he lays a cornerstone of Christian theology.

AUTHOR AND DATE

The author of this letter identifies himself as "Paul, a bondservant of Jesus Christ, called to be an apostle" (1:1), and the epistle contains a number of references that align with known details about his life. The doctrine in the book is also typical of Paul, including his explanations of justification by faith (see 3:20–22), the use of spiritual gifts in the church (see 12:3–8), and taking care of those in need (see 15:25–28). For these reasons and more, the leaders of the early church were nearly unanimous in their acceptance of his authorship. References in the New Testament (specifically in Acts and 1 and 2 Corinthians) suggest that Paul wrote the letter while he was residing in Corinth during his third missionary journey. Based on Paul's travel plans and the timetable for navigating the Mediterranean Sea, this means he likely wrote the letter in the fall of AD 57.

BACKGROUND AND SETTING

Little is known about the origin of the church in Rome, including who founded it or when it was established. Some scholars suggest that new believers who witnessed the coming of the Holy Spirit on the Day of Pentecost in Jerusalem returned to Rome to start a congregation. Little also is known about the believers themselves in Rome, yet it is clear from Paul's opening words in his letter that they were a well-established community and known for their faith (see 1:8–10). Paul's knowledge of the Roman church came secondhand, for when he wrote the letter, he had yet to visit them (see 1:11–12). This was not due to a lack of interest, for ministering in Rome was one of the apostle's greatest desires. The Holy Spirit, however, had other plans for him. When Paul did make it to Rome, it was as a prisoner, waiting to stand trial before Caesar.

KEY THEMES

Several key themes are prominent in Paul's letter to the Romans. The first is that *justification (being made righteous before God) comes by faith alone in Christ.* Paul explains that *all* have sinned and stand condemned for failing to live up to God's standard of righteousness (see 1:19–3:20). Some had claimed the way to achieve this righteousness (and thus attain salvation) was by following the Old Testament law. However, while Paul agrees the law is good for teaching about God's holiness, our sin, and God's ultimate plan for redemption, he concludes the law itself is powerless to save. Only faith in Jesus can bring salvation—it cannot be earned through good works or obedience to the law (see 3:21–5:21). Justification is therefore a gift from God that He makes available to us through the death and resurrection of His Son.

A second theme is that *God calls us to lead sanctified lives* (see 6:1–8:39). To be *sanctified* means to live according to God's design and purpose. God calls us to be holy and set apart from the world to do His work. However, even though we are no longer slaves to sin, we still have a sinful nature that resides within us. This creates a constant struggle between our desire to live godly lives and our desire to indulge our baser instincts. The Holy Spirit, who dwells within us, is our constant and powerful ally in this lifelong battle.

A third theme is that *God is sovereign and His plans never fail* (see 9:1–11:36). Some people in Paul's day were claiming that God's purposes had "failed" with Israel because the nation had generally rejected Jesus as their promised Messiah. Paul counters this argument by first reminding his readers that God is sovereign and does not always share His plans with humanity. Further, he explains that God has *always* had a plan for Israel— and these plans have not concluded even though they have not accepted Christ. Paul calls on the Gentile believers to not be proud but to remember they have been "grafted in" to God's greater plan for humanity.

A fourth theme is that *believers in Christ need to walk in righteousness* (see 12:1–15:13). The apostle Paul believed that when we receive the gift of God's salvation, it naturally produces a change within us—including a desire to turn away from our former lives of sin. The Holy Spirit comes to dwell within us and bestows gifts that will not only help us to lead a holy life but will also help us to serve and support other members in the church. Our new lives in Christ give us a new attitude on how we view those in authority, how we love our neighbors, how we work for Christ until His return, and how we accept and love others without judging them.

KEY APPLICATIONS

Many scholars today regard Romans as the greatest of Paul's letters and one of the foundational documents of Christianity. Paul addresses various topics, but all point to the truth that a loving God has offered salvation to a sinful humanity through the death and resurrection of His own Son. Reading the letter often feels like being swept along in a rapids, but in the end it leads us to the conclusion that we serve a God who is always merciful to us and always faithful to fulfill His plans for us. He has offered freedom from sin to anyone who accepts the sacrifice of Jesus. His grace and power are available to all who believe!

NOT ASHAMED OF THE GOSPEL

Romans 1:1–32

GETTING STARTED

What are some reasons that people give for *not* wanting to share the gospel of Christ?

SETTING THE STAGE

As we begin this study, let's consider why the letter of Romans is important to us today. First, there is an *intellectual* reason. In Romans, the apostle tackles many of the deepest issues of Christian thought and challenges our thinking. Not only does every sentence in Romans overflow with meaning, but in some places even a single *word* may suggest a profound idea. We can't study the letter to the Romans casually. We have to study it intentionally.

Second, there is a *doctrinal* reason for studying Romans. In almost every chapter, Paul engages in some major doctrinal discussion. And he doesn't waste any time getting into his comprehensive teaching about the gospel—he starts right in the first chapter by tackling the doctrines of the resurrection, Christ's deity, Christ's humanity, faith, and divine judgment.

Third, there is a *spiritual* reason. With the words of Paul's letter, we learn the reality of sin and its destructive consequences. We discover what it means to be redeemed and to be related to God. We uncover how to be filled with and controlled by the power of the Holy Spirit. Romans shows us how to live a life of loyalty, love, and obedience to Jesus Christ.

Fourth, there is a *practical* reason for studying Romans. If we truly know in our hearts and minds what Paul teaches in this short letter, we won't get caught up in misleading doctrine or teachings. The truth we find in Romans enables us to instantly recognize something that doesn't fit with that truth—and compels us to share what we've discovered with others. The teachings we find in Romans thus provide us with a great place to build our understanding of the truth so we can share it unashamedly with others.

EXPLORING THE TEXT

Paul's Greeting (Romans 1:1–7)

¹ Paul, a bondservant of Jesus Christ, called to be an apostle, separated to the gospel of God ² which He promised before through His prophets in the Holy Scriptures, ³ concerning His Son Jesus Christ

our Lord, who was born of the seed of David according to the flesh, [4] and declared to be the Son of God with power according to the Spirit of holiness, by the resurrection from the dead. [5] Through Him we have received grace and apostleship for obedience to the faith among all nations for His name, [6] among whom you also are the called of Jesus Christ.

[7] To all who are in Rome, beloved of God, called to be saints:

Grace to you and peace from God our Father and the Lord Jesus Christ.

---

1. How does Paul describe himself to his Roman fellow believers (see verses 1–2)? What do you think he implies by describing himself in this manner?

_____

_____

_____

_____

_____

_____

_____

2. How does Paul describe his appointment as a messenger of the gospel (see verses 5–6)?

_____

_____

_____

_____

_____

_____

_____

_____

Paul's Desire to Visit Rome (Romans 1:8–15)

⁸ First, I thank my God through Jesus Christ for you all, that your faith is spoken of throughout the whole world. ⁹ For God is my witness, whom I serve with my spirit in the gospel of His Son, that without ceasing I make mention of you always in my prayers, ¹⁰ making request if, by some means, now at last I may find a way in the will of God to come to you. ¹¹ For I long to see you, that I may impart to you some spiritual gift, so that you may be established—¹² that is, that I may be encouraged together with you by the mutual faith both of you and me.

¹³ Now I do not want you to be unaware, brethren, that I often planned to come to you (but was hindered until now), that I might have some fruit among you also, just as among the other Gentiles. ¹⁴ I am a debtor both to Greeks and to barbarians, both to wise and to unwise. ¹⁵ So, as much as is in me, I am ready to preach the gospel to you who are in Rome also.

3. What had Paul learned about this congregation in Rome (whom he had never visited)? What does he state is his prayer and desire concerning them (see verses 8–12)?

4. Why did Paul desire to visit the Roman believers (see verses 13–15)?

_____

_____

_____

_____

_____

_____

_____

_____

_____

_____

_____

God's Wrath Against Sinful Humanity (Romans 1:16–23)

16 For I am not ashamed of the gospel of Christ, for it is the power of God to salvation for everyone who believes, for the Jew first and also for the Greek. 17 For in it the righteousness of God is revealed from faith to faith; as it is written, "The just shall live by faith."

18 For the wrath of God is revealed from heaven against all ungodliness and unrighteousness of men, who suppress the truth in unrighteousness, 19 because what may be known of God is manifest in them, for God has shown it to them. 20 For since the creation of the world His invisible attributes are clearly seen, being understood by the things that are made, even His eternal power and Godhead, so that they are without excuse, 21 because, although they knew God, they did not glorify Him as God, nor were thankful, but became futile in their thoughts, and their foolish hearts were darkened. 22 Professing to be wise, they became fools, 23 and changed the glory of the incorruptible God into an image made like corruptible man—and birds and four-footed animals and creeping things.

5. What does Paul mean when he says that he is not "ashamed" of the gospel? What reasons does he give for his zeal in sharing the gospel (see verses 16–17)?

_____

_____

_____

_____

_____

_____

_____

6. Paul begins to explain his desire for sharing the gospel of Christ by establishing the fact that people are sinful and in need of salvation from God. What are some of the reasons Paul gives for why humanity is worthy of God's wrath (see verses 18–23)?

_____

_____

_____

_____

_____

_____

_____

The Consequences of Sin (Romans 1:24–32)

24 Therefore God also gave them up to uncleanness, in the lusts of their hearts, to dishonor their bodies among themselves, 25 who exchanged the truth of God for the lie, and worshiped and served the creature rather than the Creator, who is blessed forever. Amen.

26 For this reason God gave them up to vile passions. For even their women exchanged the natural use for what is against nature.

[27] Likewise also the men, leaving the natural use of the woman, burned in their lust for one another, men with men committing what is shameful, and receiving in themselves the penalty of their error which was due.

[28] And even as they did not like to retain God in their knowledge, God gave them over to a debased mind, to do those things which are not fitting; [29] being filled with all unrighteousness, sexual immorality, wickedness, covetousness, maliciousness; full of envy, murder, strife, deceit, evil-mindedness; they are whisperers, [30] backbiters, haters of God, violent, proud, boasters, inventors of evil things, disobedient to parents, [31] undiscerning, untrustworthy, unloving, unforgiving, unmerciful; [32] who, knowing the righteous judgment of God, that those who practice such things are deserving of death, not only do the same but also approve of those who practice them.

7. How did God choose to respond to humanity's rejection of Him and His truth? Why do you think God chose to respond in this way (see verses 24–27)?

8. What consequences did God allow to happen as a result of people's sin and debased minds? What conclusion does Paul reach about those who choose this path (see verses 28–32)?

_____

_____

_____

_____

_____

_____

REVIEWING THE STORY

Paul reminded the believers in Rome that God had called him and set him apart to be an apostle of the gospel. He had received news of their faithfulness—likely in the face of persecution—and noted that their example had inspired others. Paul proclaimed he was not ashamed of his role as a minister of the gospel and expressed his desire to be with them in person. He then began his first argument, setting up the case that humanity is sinful and in need of a Savior. He also issued a warning to the unrighteous who suppress God's truth—stating that if they do not acknowledge Him, He will give them over to their sin.

9. How does Paul describe the coming of Christ into the world (see Romans 1:2–4)?

_____

_____

_____

_____

_____

_____

10. Why was Paul especially grateful for the church in Rome (see Romans 1:8)?

_____

_____

_____

_____

_____

_____

_____

11. Why did Paul boldly embrace his role as minister of the gospel (see Romans 1:16–17)?

_____

_____

_____

_____

_____

_____

_____

12. What two decisions does Paul say lie at the heart of unrighteousness—refusing to acknowledge God's truth and follow Him in obedience (see Romans 1:25)?

_____

_____

_____

_____

_____

_____

_____

APPLYING THE MESSAGE

13. In what ways do you believe that God has set you apart to share the gospel?

_____

_____

_____

_____

_____

_____

14. What consequences have you seen in your own life when you reject God's truth?

_____

_____

_____

_____

_____

_____

_____

REFLECTING ON THE MEANING

Paul's motivation for writing the letter to the Romans may be summed up in these words: "For I am not ashamed of the gospel of Christ, for it is the power of God to salvation for everyone who believes, for the Jew first and also for the Greek" (Romans 1:16). To Paul, the gospel was _everything_. For this reason, he wouldn't allow _anything_—neither the fear of being humiliated nor the threat of being persecuted—to stop him from telling people about the life-saving, transformational power that only comes through faith in Jesus.

Paul's desire to teach the truth of the gospel and see people's lives changed compelled him to travel, write, and preach. But he wasn't always able to go where he wanted. In a parenthetical statement, Paul told the Roman believers that he had often planned to visit "but was hindered" (verse 13). His statement raises a pertinent question: *How can Christians be hindered in sharing the gospel with other people?*

First, we may be hindered by our own unwillingness to obey God and boldly share our faith. We give excuses or fear what people will think about us. Paul encourages us to focus not on ourselves but on the transforming power of the gospel to change people's lives.

Second, we can be hindered from moving to a new place of ministry by an unfinished obligation. Sometimes we are prevented from doing something new because we have not yet completed what God has already assigned us to do. In Paul's case, he wanted to go to Rome, but the Lord still had work for him to do in Asia Minor and in Greece (see Romans 15:19–23).

Third, we may be hindered because of an unprincipled opponent. In 1 Thessalonians 2:18, Paul described a similar dilemma with the Thessalonian church. He said, in effect, "Satan hindered me from coming." Sometimes, it is our enemy who hinders us.

Fourth, Christians may be hindered by an unparalleled opportunity. In the book of Acts, we read how Paul had planned to preach the gospel in Asia, but he and his companions "were forbidden by the Holy Spirit to preach the word in Asia. After they had come to Mysia, they tried to go into Bithynia, but the Spirit did not permit them" (16:6–7). Paul's reasons for not going into Asia came from God's guidance—not from his own pride or shame or rebellion.

In the same way, God will sometimes allow us to be hindered from one ministry opportunity because of a different opportunity He has for us. But He wants us to be willing to share the gospel with other people no matter where we are or what we are going through. When our hearts are willing, the Lord is able to accomplish in us His "good and acceptable and perfect will" (Romans 12:2).

Journaling Your Response

What are some "hindrances" that you are facing right now in your ministry to others? Which of these four reasons do you feel best represent the cause of that hinderance?

THE STATE OF HUMANITY

Romans 2:1–3:31

GETTING STARTED

What are some doubts or questions you have raised about God's plan for your life?

_____

_____

_____

_____

_____

_____

_____

_____

_____

_____

_____

_____

_____

_____

_____

_____

_____

_____

_____

SETTING THE STAGE

In the opening of his letter to the Romans, the apostle Paul sets forth the argument that all humanity is guilty of committing sin and thus deserving of God's wrath. In writing this, Paul understood that some of the Jewish people of his day believed that because they were children of Abraham, they had a special kind of "diplomatic immunity" from God's judgment. They did not like Paul's teaching that Jews and Gentiles were equally under God's wrath because of sin. Some had even started to accuse Paul of teaching a faith-only religion that led to immorality.

Paul knew their arguments. In this next section of his letter, he determines to deal with their disapproval before their disgruntled objections could gain any credibility. He explains how God doesn't show any favoritism. He shows how God judges both Jews and Gentiles alike. He notes that God extends His grace based not on peoples' good works or adherence to any religious ritual or law—but solely on whether they place their faith in Jesus Christ.

As we will see, Paul chooses to focus on three specific questions that his Jewish opponents had raised. The first involves God's faithfulness and human unfaithfulness. The second involves God's righteousness and human unrighteousness. The third involves God's truthfulness and human untruthfulness. By anticipating and addressing these questions, Paul sets an example for all believers. His approach aligns with Peter's counsel to "always be ready to give a defense to everyone who asks you a reason for the hope that is in you" (1 Peter 3:15).

EXPLORING THE TEXT

God's Righteous Judgment (Romans 2:1–16)

¹ Therefore you are inexcusable, O man, whoever you are who judge, for in whatever you judge another you condemn yourself;

for you who judge practice the same things. [2] But we know that the judgment of God is according to truth against those who practice such things. [3] And do you think this, O man, you who judge those practicing such things, and doing the same, that you will escape the judgment of God? [4] Or do you despise the riches of His goodness, forbearance, and longsuffering, not knowing that the goodness of God leads you to repentance? [5] But in accordance with your hardness and your impenitent heart you are treasuring up for yourself wrath in the day of wrath and revelation of the righteous judgment of God, [6] who "will render to each one according to his deeds": [7] eternal life to those who by patient continuance in doing good seek for glory, honor, and immortality; [8] but to those who are self-seeking and do not obey the truth, but obey unrighteousness—indignation and wrath, [9] tribulation and anguish, on every soul of man who does evil, of the Jew first and also of the Greek; [10] but glory, honor, and peace to everyone who works what is good, to the Jew first and also to the Greek. [11] For there is no partiality with God.

[12] For as many as have sinned without law will also perish without law, and as many as have sinned in the law will be judged by the law [13] (for not the hearers of the law are just in the sight of God, but the doers of the law will be justified; [14] for when Gentiles, who do not have the law, by nature do the things in the law, these, although not having the law, are a law to themselves, [15] who show the work of the law written in their hearts, their conscience also bearing witness, and between themselves their thoughts accusing or else excusing them) [16] in the day when God will judge the secrets of men by Jesus Christ, according to my gospel.

---

1. Paul employs a common device in this passage (known as a *diatribe*) in which he sets up an imagined opponent so he can counter any objection to what he has just stated. Why does Paul condemn this "opponent" for judging himself better than others? In what ways does Paul say that this person is deceiving himself (see verses 1–6)?

_____

_____

_____

_____

_____

2. The Jewish people of Paul's day had the law—but no one had succeeded in keeping it besides Christ. What does Paul say about those who "do not have the law"? How does God judge the Gentiles, given that they do not have the law (see verses 13–16)?

_____

_____

_____

_____

All Considered Guilty (Romans 2:17–29)

17 Indeed you are called a Jew, and rest on the law, and make your boast in God, 18 and know His will, and approve the things that are excellent, being instructed out of the law, 19 and are confident that you yourself are a guide to the blind, a light to those who are in darkness, 20 an instructor of the foolish, a teacher of babes, having the form of knowledge and truth in the law. 21 You, therefore, who teach another, do you not teach yourself? You who preach that a man should not steal, do you steal? 22 You who say, "Do not commit adultery," do you commit adultery? You who abhor idols, do you rob temples? 23 You who make your boast in the law, do you dishonor God through breaking the law? 24 For "the name of God is blasphemed among the Gentiles because of you," as it is written.

²⁵ For circumcision is indeed profitable if you keep the law; but if you are a breaker of the law, your circumcision has become uncircumcision. ²⁶ Therefore, if an uncircumcised man keeps the righteous requirements of the law, will not his uncircumcision be counted as circumcision? ²⁷ And will not the physically uncircumcised, if he fulfills the law, judge you who, even with your written code and circumcision, are a transgressor of the law? ²⁸ For he is not a Jew who is one outwardly, nor is circumcision that which is outward in the flesh; ²⁹ but he is a Jew who is one inwardly; and circumcision is that of the heart, in the Spirit, not in the letter; whose praise is not from men but from God.

---

3. Paul now turns to the issue of whether the Jewish people had an advantage over their non-Jewish counterparts when it came to God's judgment for sin. How does he say these Jews viewed themselves? In what did they place their confidence (see verses 17–20)?

4. Circumcision was a rite that separated the Jewish people from the world and symbolized that they belonged to God. What does Paul say about the value of this practice? What truly is the mark that a person belongs to God (see verses 25–29)?

No One Is Righteous (Romans 3:1–20)

¹ What advantage then has the Jew, or what is the profit of circumcision? ² Much in every way! Chiefly because to them were committed the oracles of God. ³ For what if some did not believe? Will their unbelief make the faithfulness of God without effect? ⁴ Certainly not! Indeed, let God be true but every man a liar. As it is written:

> "That You may be justified in Your words,
> And may overcome when You are judged."

⁵ But if our unrighteousness demonstrates the righteousness of God, what shall we say? Is God unjust who inflicts wrath? (I speak as a man.) ⁶ Certainly not! For then how will God judge the world?

⁷ For if the truth of God has increased through my lie to His glory, why am I also still judged as a sinner? ⁸ And why not say, "Let us do evil that good may come"?—as we are slanderously reported and as some affirm that we say. Their condemnation is just.

⁹ What then? Are we better than they? Not at all. For we have previously charged both Jews and Greeks that they are all under sin.

¹⁰ As it is written:

> "There is none righteous, no, not one;
> ¹¹ There is none who understands;
> There is none who seeks after God.
> ¹² They have all turned aside;
> They have together become unprofitable;
> There is none who does good, no, not one."
> ¹³ "Their throat is an open tomb;
> With their tongues they have practiced deceit";
> "The poison of asps is under their lips";
> ¹⁴ "Whose mouth is full of cursing and bitterness."
> ¹⁵ "Their feet are swift to shed blood;

¹⁶ Destruction and misery are in their ways;

¹⁷ And the way of peace they have not known."

¹⁸ "There is no fear of God before their eyes."

¹⁹ Now we know that whatever the law says, it says to those who are under the law, that every mouth may be stopped, and all the world may become guilty before God. ²⁰ Therefore by the deeds of the law no flesh will be justified in His sight, for by the law is the knowledge of sin.

---

5. What advantages had the Jewish people received that was not given to other peoples? How had God proven Himself faithful—in spite of His peoples' unfaithfulness (see verses 1–4)?

_____

_____

_____

_____

_____

_____

_____

6. How does Paul back up his previous claim that everyone—both Jew _and_ Gentile alike—are guilty of the penalty of sin? What does the law reveal about us (see verses 9–20)?

_____

_____

_____

_____

_____

_____

_____

God's Righteousness Through Faith (Romans 3:21–31)

21 But now the righteousness of God apart from the law is revealed, being witnessed by the Law and the Prophets, 22 even the righteousness of God, through faith in Jesus Christ, to all and on all who believe. For there is no difference; 23 for all have sinned and fall short of the glory of God, 24 being justified freely by His grace through the redemption that is in Christ Jesus, 25 whom God set forth as a propitiation by His blood, through faith, to demonstrate His righteousness, because in His forbearance God had passed over the sins that were previously committed, 26 to demonstrate at the present time His righteousness, that He might be just and the justifier of the one who has faith in Jesus.

27 Where is boasting then? It is excluded. By what law? Of works? No, but by the law of faith. 28 Therefore we conclude that a man is justified by faith apart from the deeds of the law. 29 Or is He the God of the Jews only? Is He not also the God of the Gentiles? Yes, of the Gentiles also, 30 since there is one God who will justify the circumcised by faith and the uncircumcised through faith. 31 Do we then make void the law through faith? Certainly not! On the contrary, we establish the law.

7. Paul uses the words "but now" to indicate that the world has entered into a new era of salvation brought by the sacrifice of Jesus on the cross. What does Paul say is true of every person's nature? Given this, what is required to escape the penalty of sin (see verses 21–26)?

8. Paul again refers to the Jews who had "boasted" they had received special privileges from God because they had been given the law. How does Paul respond (see verses 27–31)?

_____

_____

_____

_____

_____

Reviewing the Story

Paul warned that the Jewish people who judged the Gentiles would themselves be judged because they practiced the same kind of sins. However, unlike the self-appointed Jewish judges, God was impartial and would deal with the sin of all equally. Paul pointed out the hypocrisy in those who believed they had received special privileges from God just by being a member of the Jewish race—though he did concede the Jewish people had been given a great privilege by receiving the word and laws of God. Paul also noted that God was faithful to His plan for salvation and His people, even when they were unfaithful to Him and rejected that plan. All have sinned, so God chose to send His Son into the world to pay the penalty of that sin for all. No amount of good works can make a person righteous. Salvation comes only by accepting the righteousness that is in Christ—and putting our faith completely in Him.

9. What leads people to repentance (see Romans 2:4)?

_____

_____

_____

_____

_____

10. What impact did the hypocrisy of the Jews have on other people (see Romans 2:24)?

_____

_____

_____

_____

11. Paul states that the law cannot justify us—but what does he say that it _can_ do (see Romans 3:20)?

_____

_____

_____

_____

12. What message did Paul deliver to those who believed their obedience to the law would earn God's favor (see Romans 3:22–23)?

_____

_____

_____

_____

APPLYING THE MESSAGE

13. What should you do when you are tempted to judge another person?

_____

_____

_____

_____

_____

14. How would you explain the truth that "all have sinned and fall short of the glory of God" (Romans 3:23) to someone who believes being a good person will get them into heaven?

REFLECTING ON THE MEANING

In this section, Paul identifies three truths about God's righteousness. First, God's plan of salvation *eliminates human pride* (see 3:27–28). No one who reaches heaven will be there boasting, "Let me tell you all the great things I did to get here." Everyone enters heaven solely based on the grace of God. For this reason, we can be excited we are Christians, but we shouldn't walk around boasting about the good we have done. The truth is we haven't done anything but *believe*.

Second, God's plan of salvation *eliminates human prejudice* (see 3:29–30). God isn't prejudiced and does not show favoritism toward one person, people group, or nation. The gospel does not relate that there are two ways to be saved—one for the Jews and one for the Gentiles. There is only one cross. There is only one Savior. Everyone comes to the cross the same way—through the blood of Jesus Christ. God's plan of salvation thus does away with all racial and ethnic trappings.

Third, God's plan of salvation *eliminates human presumption* (see 3:31). Paul anticipated his readers would ask: *If we are justified by faith, does that make the law meaningless?* The answer is that God never does *anything* that is meaningless. Faith upholds the law by assigning it a proper place under God's purpose and plan. The law reveals our need for Christ, which means there is no conflict between the law and justification. The law was an important part of God's plan of salvation, for it helps us realize how desperately we need what God alone can provide.

Journaling Your Response

What would you say to someone who accused you of being narrow-minded in your belief that there is only one way to salvation—through your faith in the sacrifice of Christ for your sin?

JUSTIFICATION THROUGH FAITH

Romans 4:1–5:21

GETTING STARTED

Who are some examples of the Christian faith that stand out to you? What about their stories inspires you to likewise pursue a life of faith in God?

SETTING THE STAGE

As we have discussed, many Jews in the first century had wrongly concluded they were superior to the Gentiles because they had been born Jewish. They believed they had been given a form of "advantage" before God on the basis of their race—simply because they could trace their ancestry back to Abraham. However, as Paul notes, *all* are guilty of sin before God.

In this next section of his letter, Paul sets out to further expose the flaw in this line of thinking. He stresses that a person is *not* justified before God just for being born Jewish, nor does God accept anyone based on anything that person has done or anything from which he or she has abstained. God's acceptance and justification come through *faith* in Jesus Christ alone. God counts people as righteous because of His *grace* alone.

This was a hard lesson for Paul's generation to accept—and it has been difficult for all succeeding generations to accept as well. Someone has even said that while *Amazing Grace* is a favorite hymn, most people do not subscribe to the message that it conveys. We are a do-it-yourself society—much as the people were in Paul's day.

Paul's thesis can be summed up by his statement, "Therefore we conclude that a man is justified by faith apart from the deeds of the law" (Romans 3:28). In other words, a person is justified *without* works—apart from anything he or she can do. Paul will go on to draw on two illustrations to prove this point. He chooses no lesser examples than the Jews' most famous patriarch, Abraham, and their most famous monarch, David.

EXPLORING THE TEXT

Abraham Justified by Faith (Romans 4:1–12)

¹ What then shall we say that Abraham our father has found according to the flesh? ² For if Abraham was justified by works, he has something to boast about, but not before God. ³ For what does the Scripture say? "Abraham believed God, and it was accounted to

him for righteousness." ⁴ Now to him who works, the wages are not counted as grace but as debt.

⁵ But to him who does not work but believes on Him who justifies the ungodly, his faith is accounted for righteousness, ⁶ just as David also describes the blessedness of the man to whom God imputes righteousness apart from works:

⁷ "Blessed are those whose lawless deeds are forgiven,
And whose sins are covered;
⁸ Blessed is the man to whom the LORD shall not impute sin."

⁹ Does this blessedness then come upon the circumcised only, or upon the uncircumcised also? For we say that faith was accounted to Abraham for righteousness. ¹⁰ How then was it accounted? While he was circumcised, or uncircumcised? Not while circumcised, but while uncircumcised. ¹¹ And he received the sign of circumcision, a seal of the righteousness of the faith which he had while still uncircumcised, that he might be the father of all those who believe, though they are uncircumcised, that righteousness might be imputed to them also, ¹² and the father of circumcision to those who not only are of the circumcision, but who also walk in the steps of the faith which our father Abraham had while still uncircumcised.

---

1. In Paul's day, the Jewish people looked to Abraham as an example of righteousness for his faithfulness and obedience to God. But why does Paul say that even Abraham does not have cause to boast in his own good works, actions, and behaviors (see verses 1–4)?

2. Paul states that God declared Abraham to be righteous *before* he went through the practice of circumcision. How does Paul use this fact to support his claim that it is *faith* rather than *works* that leads to righteousness before God (see verses 9–12)?

The Promise Granted Through Faith (Romans 4:13–25)

¹³ For the promise that he would be the heir of the world was not to Abraham or to his seed through the law, but through the righteousness of faith. ¹⁴ For if those who are of the law are heirs, faith is made void and the promise made of no effect, ¹⁵ because the law brings about wrath; for where there is no law there is no transgression.

¹⁶ Therefore it is of faith that it might be according to grace, so that the promise might be sure to all the seed, not only to those who are of the law, but also to those who are of the faith of Abraham, who is the father of us all ¹⁷ (as it is written, "I have made you a father of many nations") in the presence of Him whom he believed—God, who gives life to the dead and calls those things which do not exist as though they did; ¹⁸ who, contrary to hope, in hope believed, so that he became the father of many nations, according to what was spoken, "So shall your descendants be." ¹⁹ And not being weak in faith, he did not consider his own body, already dead (since he was about a hundred years old), and the deadness of Sarah's womb. ²⁰ He did not waver at the promise of God through unbelief, but was strengthened in faith, giving glory to God, ²¹ and being fully convinced that what He had promised He was also able to perform. ²² And therefore "it was accounted to him for righteousness."

²³ Now it was not written for his sake alone that it was imputed to him, ²⁴ but also for us. It shall be imputed to us who believe in Him who raised up Jesus our Lord from the dead, ²⁵ who was delivered up because of our offenses, and was raised because of our justification.

---

3. How does Paul say that Abraham received the promise that he and Sarah would give birth to a son? Why was Abraham's faith so critical in this process (see verses 13–15)?

_____

_____

_____

_____

_____

4. What are some of the ways that Abraham demonstrated his faith in God? What was the ultimate result of these demonstrations of faith (see verses 19–22)?

_____

_____

_____

_____

_____

Peace and Hope Through Christ (Romans 5:1–11)

¹ Therefore, having been justified by faith, we have peace with God through our Lord Jesus Christ, ² through whom also we have access

by faith into this grace in which we stand, and rejoice in hope of the glory of God. [3] And not only that, but we also glory in tribulations, knowing that tribulation produces perseverance; [4] and perseverance, character; and character, hope. [5] Now hope does not disappoint, because the love of God has been poured out in our hearts by the Holy Spirit who was given to us.

[6] For when we were still without strength, in due time Christ died for the ungodly. [7] For scarcely for a righteous man will one die; yet perhaps for a good man someone would even dare to die. [8] But God demonstrates His own love toward us, in that while we were still sinners, Christ died for us. [9] Much more then, having now been justified by His blood, we shall be saved from wrath through Him. [10] For if when we were enemies we were reconciled to God through the death of His Son, much more, having been reconciled, we shall be saved by His life. [11] And not only that, but we also rejoice in God through our Lord Jesus Christ, through whom we have now received the reconciliation.

5. How can believers find peace with God? Why can believers even be joyful during times of intense trials and tribulations (see verses 1–5)?

6. How did God demonstrate that He is the One who seeks out the lost and rescues them from their sin? In what ways was Jesus' sacrifice on the cross the greatest demonstration of God's love for us (see verses 6–11)?

Death in Adam, Life in Christ (Romans 5:12–21)

[12] Therefore, just as through one man sin entered the world, and death through sin, and thus death spread to all men, because all sinned— [13] (For until the law sin was in the world, but sin is not imputed when there is no law. [14] Nevertheless death reigned from Adam to Moses, even over those who had not sinned according to the likeness of the transgression of Adam, who is a type of Him who was to come. [15] But the free gift is not like the offense. For if by the one man's offense many died, much more the grace of God and the gift by the grace of the one Man, Jesus Christ, abounded to many. [16] And the gift is not like that which came through the one who sinned. For the judgment which came from one offense resulted in condemnation, but the free gift which came from many offenses resulted in justification. [17] For if by the one man's offense death reigned through the one, much more those who receive abundance of grace and of the gift of righteousness will reign in life through the One, Jesus Christ.)

[18] Therefore, as through one man's offense judgment came to all men, resulting in condemnation, even so through one Man's righteous act the free gift came to all men, resulting in justification of life. [19] For as by one man's disobedience many were made sinners, so also by one Man's obedience many will be made righteous.

²⁰ Moreover the law entered that the offense might abound. But where sin abounded, grace abounded much more, ²¹ so that as sin reigned in death, even so grace might reign through righteousness to eternal life through Jesus Christ our Lord.

---

7. Paul compares and contrasts two men in this passage. What does Paul say occurred as a result of the first man's actions (see verses 12–14)? What happened as a result of the second man's actions (see verse 15)?

_____

_____

_____

_____

8. What conclusion does Paul reach about the act of righteousness that Jesus performed on the cross? What impact does that act have on us today (see verses 18–21)?

_____

_____

_____

_____

REVIEWING THE STORY

Paul illustrated the concept of justification by drawing on the Old Testament example of Abraham. Paul notes that God counted him as righteous *before* he was circumcised—which means it wasn't the *act* of circumcision that made him righteous but rather his *faith* in God. In the same way, God forgave David's sin—and granted him justification—through David's faith and not his works. Today, we are to follow the examples of these men and seek justification through faith rather than works. When we do, we can be confident that we are at peace with God, have access to His presence, and will grow in perseverance, character, and hope.

9. How are the wages of "him who works" counted (see Romans 4:4)?

10. Why did Jesus go to the cross? What was the result of His resurrection? (see Romans 4:25)?

11. What is the process by which tribulation will lead to hope (see Romans 5:3–4)?

12. What connection does Paul make between the law, sin, and grace (see Romans 5:20–21)?

APPLYING THE MESSAGE

13. Why is it so important to realize that salvation comes through your faith in God and not your works for God? How should this truth impact the way you lead your life?

_____

_____

_____

_____

_____

14. Paul writes that God demonstrated His love "in that while we were still sinners, Christ died for us" (5:8). What does this act of sacrificial love mean to you personally?

_____

_____

_____

_____

_____

REFLECTING ON THE MEANING

In this section of Paul's letter, he states that believers in Christ can not only _endure_ trials but can actually _glory_ in them because of the positive attributes they produce. Paul was eminently qualified to talk about suffering and trials, for he was continually exposed to them over the course of his ministry. Yet his take on those Christian realities—that one can _rejoice_ in them—can seem counterintuitive. How can one actually be joyful during times of pain?

Paul did not make this claim because he was masochistic and enjoyed going through suffering. Rather, by paying careful attention to what God was doing in the midst of tribulation, he had come to learn the process.

What we know makes a big difference when we are going through trials. If we don't know anything about God or how He uses trials for our benefit, we are going to have a hard time in the midst of them.

Paul identifies three results of trials that have the potential to change the way we think about suffering. The first is that *tribulation produces perseverance.* Perseverance is the ability to remain stable in the midst of pressure. Many people's first reaction to tribulation is to flee, to run and hide, to try to escape it. But Paul urged us to fight that instinct. When we stand and face tribulation—with God's help—our resolve toughens, our confidence grows, our knowledge expands, and our faith deepens. When our faith endures hardship, we find that our faith comes through stronger because of the testing.

Second, *perseverance produces character.* When we persevere, we come out the other side of the tribulation with a strength of character that we did not possess before—what someone called "tried integrity." James echoes the point: "My brethren, count it all joy when you fall into various trials, knowing that the testing of your faith produces patience. But let patience have its perfect work, that you may be perfect and complete, lacking nothing" (1:2–4). As we persevere we become "veterans" in the faith, confident in our knowledge that God will be with us during the trial and will ultimately use it to deepen our trust in Him.

Third, *character produces hope.* Our character strengthens our hope in God. We come to realize that God's grace is sufficient for us. Paul came to this very conclusion after an intense time of trial in his own life. In his second letter to the Corinthians, he explained, "[God] said to me, 'My grace is sufficient for you, for My strength is made perfect in weakness.' Therefore most gladly I will rather boast in my infirmities, that the power of Christ may rest upon me" (12:9). Paul had learned to "boast" in his infirmities because he recognized how God was using them.

For these reasons, when tribulation seems unrelenting, we also need to consider what God is doing in our lives as we go through them. We need to be open to the work that He wants to accomplish in us through such trials. He is on our side and always has our interests at heart.

JOURNALING YOUR RESPONSE

What will be the first thing you do the next time you face tribulation?

LESSON *four*

SPIRITUAL SLAVERY

Romans 6:1–7:25

GETTING STARTED

What would you say to someone who claimed that God's forgiveness and grace give us the freedom to do anything we want?

SETTING THE STAGE

In the first portion of Romans, the apostle Paul has dealt with what happens to us the moment we believe. He described what we were before we came to Christ and who we are now that we have believed. In this next section, he details how we are to *live* the Christian life. He discusses two theological terms that we need to understand: *justification* and *sanctification*.

Justification is our eternal position before God through Christ. In God's sight, we are justified. We are positionally perfect—but we are not practically perfect. *Sanctification* is becoming gradually, in practice, what we already are in position. In other words, we have *been* justified. But the more we walk with God, the more we *are being* sanctified.

Justification is an act; sanctification is a work. Justification is *for* us; sanctification is *in* us. Justification is a transaction; sanctification is a transformation. Justification declares the sinner righteous; sanctification makes us righteous daily in our walk with God. Justification removes all the guilt and penalty for our sin; sanctification removes the growth and power of our sin. Justification is the straight gate through which we enter the narrow way of holiness; sanctification is the way of holiness itself.

Now that we are justified in the eyes of God, we have a life to live here on earth. Every day as we walk with the Lord, we are continually becoming more holy. As we put ourselves through the disciplines of the Word of God, He is growing us to be what we already are in His sight. This is the process of sanctification.

EXPLORING THE TEXT

Dead to Sin, Alive to God (Romans 6:1–14)

¹ What shall we say then? Shall we continue in sin that grace may abound? ² Certainly not! How shall we who died to sin live any longer in it? ³ Or do you not know that as many of us as were baptized into Christ Jesus were baptized into His death? ⁴ Therefore we were buried

with Him through baptism into death, that just as Christ was raised from the dead by the glory of the Father, even so we also should walk in newness of life.

⁵ For if we have been united together in the likeness of His death, certainly we also shall be in the likeness of His resurrection, ⁶ knowing this, that our old man was crucified with Him, that the body of sin might be done away with, that we should no longer be slaves of sin. ⁷ For he who has died has been freed from sin. ⁸ Now if we died with Christ, we believe that we shall also live with Him, ⁹ knowing that Christ, having been raised from the dead, dies no more. Death no longer has dominion over Him. ¹⁰ For the death that He died, He died to sin once for all; but the life that He lives, He lives to God. ¹¹ Likewise you also, reckon yourselves to be dead indeed to sin, but alive to God in Christ Jesus our Lord.

¹² Therefore do not let sin reign in your mortal body, that you should obey it in its lusts. ¹³ And do not present your members as instruments of unrighteousness to sin, but present yourselves to God as being alive from the dead, and your members as instruments of righteousness to God. ¹⁴ For sin shall not have dominion over you, for you are not under law but under grace.

---

1. Paul's premise is that believers are identified with Jesus in His death, burial, and resurrection. Jesus bore our sin and overcame its power. In the same way, since we are in Christ, sin now has no claim or power over us. Given this, why is it impossible to take the position that we can continue in sin because of God's grace (see verses 1–5)?

2. Our former lives were put to death when we became believers in Christ. Given this fact, how does Paul say that we should now live (see verses 12–14)?

_____

_____

_____

_____

_____

_____

_____

Slaves to Righteousness (Romans 6:15–23)

15 What then? Shall we sin because we are not under law but under grace? Certainly not! 16 Do you not know that to whom you present yourselves slaves to obey, you are that one's slaves whom you obey, whether of sin leading to death, or of obedience leading to righteousness? 17 But God be thanked that though you were slaves of sin, yet you obeyed from the heart that form of doctrine to which you were delivered. 18 And having been set free from sin, you became slaves of righteousness. 19 I speak in human terms because of the weakness of your flesh. For just as you presented your members as slaves of uncleanness, and of lawlessness leading to more lawlessness, so now present your members as slaves of righteousness for holiness.

20 For when you were slaves of sin, you were free in regard to righteousness. 21 What fruit did you have then in the things of which you are now ashamed? For the end of those things is death. 22 But now having been set free from sin, and having become slaves of God, you have your fruit to holiness, and the end, everlasting life. 23 For the wages of sin is death, but the gift of God is eternal life in Christ Jesus our Lord.

3. Paul has previously stated that believers in Christ are no longer under the law. How does he respond to the claim that believers can thus do anything they want (see verses 15–18)?

_____

_____

_____

_____

_____

_____

_____

4. What "fruit" does Paul say a believer in Christ should exhibit as a result of no longer being a slave to sin (see verses 20–23)?

_____

_____

_____

_____

_____

_____

_____

_____

Freed from the Law (Romans 7:1–12)

¹ Or do you not know, brethren (for I speak to those who know the law), that the law has dominion over a man as long as he lives? ² For the woman who has a husband is bound by the law to her husband as long as he lives. But if the husband dies, she is released from the law of her husband. ³ So then if, while her husband lives, she marries another man, she will be called an adulteress; but if her husband dies, she is free from that law, so that she is no adulteress, though she

has married another man. ⁴ Therefore, my brethren, you also have become dead to the law through the body of Christ, that you may be married to another—to Him who was raised from the dead, that we should bear fruit to God. ⁵ For when we were in the flesh, the sinful passions which were aroused by the law were at work in our members to bear fruit to death. ⁶ But now we have been delivered from the law, having died to what we were held by, so that we should serve in the newness of the Spirit and not in the oldness of the letter.

⁷ What shall we say then? Is the law sin? Certainly not! On the contrary, I would not have known sin except through the law. For I would not have known covetousness unless the law had said, "You shall not covet." ⁸ But sin, taking opportunity by the commandment, produced in me all manner of evil desire. For apart from the law sin was dead. ⁹ I was alive once without the law, but when the commandment came, sin revived and I died. ¹⁰ And the commandment, which was to bring life, I found to bring death. ¹¹ For sin, taking occasion by the commandment, deceived me, and by it killed me. ¹² Therefore the law is holy, and the commandment holy and just and good.

---

5. Paul has just stated that believers are identified with Christ in His death and resurrection. Jesus' death has freed us from the power of sin *and* bondage to the law. How does Paul use the example of the widow in this passage to explain this point (see verses 1–6)?

_____

_____

_____

_____

_____

_____

_____

6. How does Paul describe the relationship between the *law* and *sin*? What specific impact did the law have on Paul's life (see verses 7–12)?

_____

_____

_____

_____

_____

_____

_____

_____

The Law Cannot Save (Romans 7:13–25)

¹³ Has then what is good become death to me? Certainly not! But sin, that it might appear sin, was producing death in me through what is good, so that sin through the commandment might become exceedingly sinful. ¹⁴ For we know that the law is spiritual, but I am carnal, sold under sin. ¹⁵ For what I am doing, I do not understand. For what I will to do, that I do not practice; but what I hate, that I do. ¹⁶ If, then, I do what I will not to do, I agree with the law that it is good. ¹⁷ But now, it is no longer I who do it, but sin that dwells in me. ¹⁸ For I know that in me (that is, in my flesh) nothing good dwells; for to will is present with me, but how to perform what is good I do not find. ¹⁹ For the good that I will to do, I do not do; but the evil I will not to do, that I practice. ²⁰ Now if I do what I will not to do, it is no longer I who do it, but sin that dwells in me.

²¹ I find then a law, that evil is present with me, the one who wills to do good. ²² For I delight in the law of God according to the inward man. ²³ But I see another law in my members, warring against the law of my mind, and bringing me into captivity to the law of sin which is in my members. ²⁴ O wretched man that I am! Who will deliver me from this body of death? ²⁵ I thank God—through Jesus Christ our Lord!

So then, with the mind I myself serve the law of God, but with the flesh the law of sin.

---

7. Paul depicts a struggle in this passage between the "law of God" and the "law of sin." How does he say this struggle plays out in his own life (see verses 14–19)?

_____

_____

_____

_____

_____

_____

8. As long as believers are in this world, they will continually face the temptation to sin. How does Paul describe this condition? What does he say is the solution (see verses 21–25)?

_____

_____

_____

_____

_____

_____

REVIEWING THE STORY

Paul anticipated the claim from his opponents that if God's grace increases when people sin, it gives them a license to keep on sinning . . . so they will receive more grace. But Paul explained that we are now *dead* to sin and have new *life* in Christ. We present ourselves to God, not to sin. Sin leads to death, while obedience leads to righteousness. As believers, we die to the law and to sin—but these two things are not in the same category. The law is holy, just, good, and reveals our sin. Sin produces death and torments believers. Paul then offered a transparent description of his own struggle with this sin for the benefit of his readers.

9. Why does sin have no dominion over believers (see Romans 6:14)?

_____

_____

_____

_____

_____

_____

10. According to Paul, everyone is a slave to one of which two things (see Romans 6:16)?

_____

_____

_____

_____

_____

11. What analogy did Paul use to explain the dominion that the law has over people (see Romans 7:1–3)?

_____

_____

_____

_____

_____

_____

12. How does Paul summarize the warring nature within himself (see Romans 7:24–25)?

_____

_____

_____

_____

_____

_____

APPLYING THE MESSAGE

13. What steps can you take to lessen the influence and power of sin in your life?

_____

_____

_____

_____

_____

_____

14. Why is it important to be transparent about our struggles with sin, as Paul was?

_____

_____

_____

_____

REFLECTING ON THE MEANING

What Paul described in this portion of his letter is something every believer has experienced—the continuing struggle to live a life that is pleasing to God. Paul frequently employs first-person pronouns through his letter and speaks from his own experience. Yet even as he refers to himself, he is also describing a condition that we all face at times.

When Paul states that we all have a carnal part of our nature (see 7:14), he is not referring to just immature believers in Christ. Rather, he is describing the most spiritual and mature Christians—himself included. The more honestly we measure ourselves against God's standard of righteousness, the more we realize just how much we fall short! As we evaluate our lives, we come to recognize and grieve over our sinfulness. We also come to recognize just how much we *all* are continually in need of God's grace.

There are at least two truths we can take away from Paul's candid assessment of his own struggles. First, *we need to face the reality of our sin.* Paul is talking here about the gut-level Christian experience. He does not try to gloss over the ugly truth, spiritualize it, or make it into something else. It's freeing for us to be able to admit, "I have shared many of those same struggles." We don't have to dodge reality or hide behind spiritual jargon. After all, if we are not real about our struggles, it won't be long before we deny those struggles exist.

Second, *it is only through the struggle that we can be stretched.* The only way a caterpillar can become a butterfly is through the process of struggling to get out of its cocoon. Certainly, we depend on Christ, but Christ puts us through the process of the struggle. And it is in that struggle that we experience growth. Most of us learn the hard way. We don't gain much knowledge or wisdom from success, but we learn a lot from defeat, discouragement, and frustration.

As Paul will soon explain, we are not left to face this struggle alone without any hope or guidance. For God has placed the Holy Spirit within us to help navigate the struggles in our lives. When we walk in the Spirit, we live by the grace and power of the Holy Spirit.

JOURNALING YOUR RESPONSE

How would you describe your own struggles with allowing the Holy Spirit to have full control in your own life?

A REVOLUTIONARY FREEDOM

Romans 8:1–39

GETTING STARTED

When have you seen God bring about something good from something that seemed bad?

SETTING THE STAGE

Up to this point, Paul has been presenting a picture of our fallen state as human beings. In this next section of Romans, the apostle now begins to outline the solution to our wretched state: the gift of the Holy Spirit in our lives. As Paul will relate, through the power of the Holy Spirit, we can be liberated from the law of sin and death. We can know that we will have the victory even as we struggle with our human propensity to sin. We can gain confidence, comfort, and hope in knowing there is "no condemnation to those who are in Christ Jesus" (Romans 8:1).

Paul mentions the Holy Spirit only once in Romans 7, while mentioning the Old Testament law and commandments almost *thirty* times. In Romans 8, however, he mentions the Holy Spirit *nineteen* times as he shifts his focus from the believer's justification through faith in Jesus to the believer's ability to live the Christian life through the empowering work of the Holy Spirit. The Holy Spirit thus plays a key role in the sanctification of believers—freeing them from the chains of sin to live lives that honor God.

Paul wants his readers to understand—without a shadow of a doubt—that they have a priceless standing before God as coheirs with Jesus and sons and daughters of God. He reminds them that they have a high calling as God's children, which includes both the call to suffer as Jesus suffered and the call to lead godly lives so they will one day be glorified just as Jesus was glorified. Through it all, Paul reminds believers in Christ of God's deep and unending love for them and the perfect purpose that He has for each of His children's lives.

EXPLORING THE TEXT

Free from Indwelling Sin (Romans 8:1–11)

¹ There is therefore now no condemnation to those who are in Christ Jesus, who do not walk according to the flesh, but according to the Spirit. ² For the law of the Spirit of life in Christ Jesus has made me

free from the law of sin and death. ³ For what the law could not do in that it was weak through the flesh, God did by sending His own Son in the likeness of sinful flesh, on account of sin: He condemned sin in the flesh, ⁴ that the righteous requirement of the law might be fulfilled in us who do not walk according to the flesh but according to the Spirit. ⁵ For those who live according to the flesh set their minds on the things of the flesh, but those who live according to the Spirit, the things of the Spirit. ⁶ For to be carnally minded is death, but to be spiritually minded is life and peace. ⁷ Because the carnal mind is enmity against God; for it is not subject to the law of God, nor indeed can be. ⁸ So then, those who are in the flesh cannot please God.

⁹ But you are not in the flesh but in the Spirit, if indeed the Spirit of God dwells in you. Now if anyone does not have the Spirit of Christ, he is not His. ¹⁰ And if Christ is in you, the body is dead because of sin, but the Spirit is life because of righteousness. ¹¹ But if the Spirit of Him who raised Jesus from the dead dwells in you, He who raised Christ from the dead will also give life to your mortal bodies through His Spirit who dwells in you.

---

1. Paul concluded the previous portion of his letter by lamenting about his wretched state and asking, "Who will deliver me from this body of death?" (7:24). What answer does he provide in this passage? What does the law of the Spirit of life bring (see 8:1–5)?

2. What does Paul say is the "proof" that we belong to God? What promises are we given as a result of having the Holy Spirit dwelling within us (see verses 9–11)?

_____

_____

_____

_____

_____

Sonship Through the Spirit (Romans 8:12–17)

¹² Therefore, brethren, we are debtors—not to the flesh, to live according to the flesh. ¹³ For if you live according to the flesh you will die; but if by the Spirit you put to death the deeds of the body, you will live. ¹⁴ For as many as are led by the Spirit of God, these are sons of God. ¹⁵ For you did not receive the spirit of bondage again to fear, but you received the Spirit of adoption by whom we cry out, "Abba, Father." ¹⁶ The Spirit Himself bears witness with our spirit that we are children of God, ¹⁷ and if children, then heirs—heirs of God and joint heirs with Christ, if indeed we suffer with Him, that we may also be glorified together.

3. Paul states that we have a *debt* or *obligation* to fulfill—but that debt is not to the flesh. How are we to live? What privileges will that bring to us (see verses 12–14)?

_____

_____

_____

_____

_____

4. What does Paul say that each of us received at the moment of our salvation? To what does the Holy Spirit bear witness in our lives (see verses 15–17)?

_____

_____

_____

_____

_____

_____

From Suffering to Glory (Romans 8:18–30)

18 For I consider that the sufferings of this present time are not worthy to be compared with the glory which shall be revealed in us. 19 For the earnest expectation of the creation eagerly waits for the revealing of the sons of God. 20 For the creation was subjected to futility, not willingly, but because of Him who subjected it in hope; 21 because the creation itself also will be delivered from the bondage of corruption into the glorious liberty of the children of God. 22 For we know that the whole creation groans and labors with birth pangs together until now. 23 Not only that, but we also who have the firstfruits of the Spirit, even we ourselves groan within ourselves, eagerly waiting for the adoption, the redemption of our body. 24 For we were saved in this hope, but hope that is seen is not hope; for why does one still hope for what he sees? 25 But if we hope for what we do not see, we eagerly wait for it with perseverance.

26 Likewise the Spirit also helps in our weaknesses. For we do not know what we should pray for as we ought, but the Spirit Himself makes intercession for us with groanings which cannot be uttered. 27 Now He who searches the hearts knows what the mind of the Spirit is, because He makes intercession for the saints according to the will of God.

²⁸ And we know that all things work together for good to those who love God, to those who are the called according to His purpose. ²⁹ For whom He foreknew, He also predestined to be conformed to the image of His Son, that He might be the firstborn among many brethren. ³⁰ Moreover whom He predestined, these He also called; whom He called, these He also justified; and whom He justified, these He also glorified.

---

5. Paul opens this section by comparing the pain of his present sufferings against the future glory that awaits him in eternity. What conclusions does he reach? What does he say all "creation itself" is waiting to receive (see verses 18–22)?

_____

_____

_____

_____

_____

_____

6. In what ways does the Holy Spirit help us in our prayers to God? What promise do we have if we love God and respond to the work of the Holy Spirit (see verses 26–30)?

_____

_____

_____

_____

_____

_____

God's Everlasting Love (Romans 8:31–39)

³¹ What then shall we say to these things? If God is for us, who can be against us? ³² He who did not spare His own Son, but delivered Him up for us all, how shall He not with Him also freely give us all things? ³³ Who shall bring a charge against God's elect? It is God who justifies. ³⁴ Who is he who condemns? It is Christ who died, and furthermore is also risen, who is even at the right hand of God, who also makes intercession for us. ³⁵ Who shall separate us from the love of Christ? Shall tribulation, or distress, or persecution, or famine, or nakedness, or peril, or sword? ³⁶ As it is written:

> "For Your sake we are killed all day long;
> We are accounted as sheep for the slaughter."

³⁷ Yet in all these things we are more than conquerors through Him who loved us. ³⁸ For I am persuaded that neither death nor life, nor angels nor principalities nor powers, nor things present nor things to come, ³⁹ nor height nor depth, nor any other created thing, shall be able to separate us from the love of God which is in Christ Jesus our Lord.

---

7. Paul now begins to expound on the incredible blessings a person receives who accepts God's offer of salvation. What are some of those blessings (see verses 31–35)?

_____

_____

_____

_____

_____

_____

8. Paul quotes Psalm 44:22 to emphasize that suffering is a normal part of life for the follower of God. However, what does he imply we should keep in mind as we are dealing with the trials of life? Of what can we be assured (see verses 36–39)?

_____

_____

_____

_____

_____

REVIEWING THE STORY

Paul celebrated what it means for a believer to have life through the Spirit—which includes freedom from the law of sin and death—and contrasted it against the perils of living in the flesh. While living in the Spirit brings freedom, living according to the flesh only leads to bondage and death. Those who accept Jesus as their Savior thus have an obligation to live according to the direction of the Holy Spirit. As we do this, we are living as children of God and joint heirs with Jesus—with all the rights and privileges that status brings. Paul also notes that our present suffering is minor when compared to the future eternal glory that awaits us. When the Holy Spirit resides within us, we can know that God will be with us in the midst of any trial, will help us in our prayers, and will enable us to conquer the attacks of our enemy.

9. What was the law powerless to do? How did God address this issue (see Romans 8:3)?

_____

_____

_____

_____

10. What two things are believers called to share in with Christ (see Romans 8:17)?

_____

_____

_____

_____

_____

_____

11. What are some of the things the Holy Spirit does in our lives (see Romans 8:26–27)?

_____

_____

_____

_____

_____

_____

12. What point does Paul make about the love of God for His children (see Romans 8:37–39)?

_____

_____

_____

_____

_____

_____

APPLYING THE MESSAGE

13. What would you add, as a reminder to yourself, to Paul's list of things that cannot separate you from God's love?

_____

_____

_____

_____

_____

_____

14. What would you say to someone in your life today who feels abandoned by God?

_____

_____

_____

_____

_____

_____

REFLECTING ON THE MEANING

Paul writes that believers "are more than conquerors" through Christ (8:37). In other words, believers are winning the *supreme battle* against their enemy in this life. They are conquerors over the strategies their spiritual opponents are waging. They are conquerors not just in the momentary struggles but also in the continual and ongoing war that is raging. The victories they are securing are of an eternal nature, with rewards that are not temporary but everlasting.

These promises allow you to say, "In Jesus Christ, I am more than a conqueror." What an amazing truth! However, to truly recognize this truth, you first have to understand what the Bible says about *who you are* in Christ—that you are "sons [and daughters] of God" (verse 14)—and know what rights and privileges that brings. After all, if you can come to accept these truths about you, you will start to act more like that person. You will begin to truly walk with confidence in this life, knowing that you have been given the ultimate victory.

Here are a few verses from the Bible that can help to remind you of your identity in Christ and the promises you have been given as a child of God:

- "But as many as received Him, to them He gave the right to become children of God, to those who believe in His name" (John 1:12).

- "Therefore, if anyone is in Christ, he is a new creation; old things have passed away; behold, all things have become new" (2 Corinthians 5:17).

- "For we are His workmanship, created in Christ Jesus for good works, which God prepared beforehand that we should walk in them" (Ephesians 2:10).

- "For our citizenship is in heaven, from which we also eagerly wait for the Savior, the Lord Jesus Christ" (Philippians 3:20).

- "You are a chosen generation, a royal priesthood, a holy nation, His own special people, that you may proclaim the praises of Him who called you out of darkness into His marvelous light" (1 Peter 2:9).

These are words that will sustain, encourage, and embolden those of us who are more than conquerors through Christ Jesus.

Journaling Your Response

What does it mean to you that you are more than a conqueror in Christ?

LESSON *six*

TRUE AND FALSE BELIEVERS

Romans 9:1–33

GETTING STARTED

What evidence have you seen in your life that God is just and fair?

SETTING THE STAGE

Paul opened his letter to the Romans by identifying the priority of the gospel: "for the Jew first and also for the Greek" (1:16). The gospel was first given to the people of Israel through the birth, ministry, death, and resurrection of Jesus. But how does the gospel of Christ—which Paul has so eloquently presented in the first eight chapters of Romans—fit in with God's plan for His chosen nation of Israel? For though it is true the gospel is for everyone, the Bible also makes it clear that God did something unique with the people of Israel. He chose them to be His own special people out of all the nations in the world (see Deuteronomy 7:6; 14:2).

This is what the apostle Paul will now address: how the Jewish nation fits into God's plan of redemption. He begins by making it clear to his fellow Jews that Judaism alone cannot bring salvation. Paul himself, prior to his conversion, had been considered great by Jewish standards. As he stated in his letter to the Philippians, "If anyone else thinks he may have confidence in the flesh, I more so: circumcised the eighth day, of the stock of Israel, of the tribe of Benjamin, a Hebrew of the Hebrews; concerning the law, a Pharisee; concerning zeal, persecuting the church; concerning the righteousness which is in the law, blameless" (3:5–6).

Yet, in his next breath, Paul said, "But what things were gain to me, these I have counted loss for Christ" (verse 7). Paul likewise understood that if his Jewish brethren—his countrymen, family members, and those who were close to him—didn't understand this, they would miss everything that God had made available to them. They would miss the *gospel*.

EXPLORING THE TEXT

Israel's Rejection of the Messiah (Romans 9:1–13)

> [1] I tell the truth in Christ, I am not lying, my conscience also bearing me witness in the Holy Spirit, [2] that I have great sorrow and continual grief in my heart. [3] For I could wish that I myself were accursed from

Christ for my brethren, my countrymen according to the flesh, [4] who are Israelites, to whom pertain the adoption, the glory, the covenants, the giving of the law, the service of God, and the promises; [5] of whom are the fathers and from whom, according to the flesh, Christ came, who is over all, the eternally blessed God. Amen.

[6] But it is not that the word of God has taken no effect. For they are not all Israel who are of Israel, [7] nor are they all children because they are the seed of Abraham; but, "In Isaac your seed shall be called." [8] That is, those who are the children of the flesh, these are not the children of God; but the children of the promise are counted as the seed. [9] For this is the word of promise: "At this time I will come and Sarah shall have a son."

[10] And not only this, but when Rebecca also had conceived by one man, even by our father Isaac [11] (for the children not yet being born, nor having done any good or evil, that the purpose of God according to election might stand, not of works but of Him who calls), [12] it was said to her, "The older shall serve the younger." [13] As it is written, "Jacob I have loved, but Esau I have hated."

---

1. Paul previously mentioned the great advantages the Jewish people received in being members of God's chosen race. Yet in this section he will point out their failings for rejecting Jesus as the Messiah. What anguish does Paul express over this (see verses 1–5)?

2. Paul draws on the examples of Abraham, Isaac, and Jacob to show that God's purposes have always involved more than just the members of the Jewish race. According to Paul, whom does God consider to be His "children of the promise" (see verses 6–13)?

_____

_____

_____

_____

_____

_____

_____

_____

_____

_____

God's Supreme Justice (Romans 9:14–21)

¹⁴ What shall we say then? Is there unrighteousness with God? Certainly not! ¹⁵ For He says to Moses, "I will have mercy on whomever I will have mercy, and I will have compassion on whomever I will have compassion." ¹⁶ So then it is not of him who wills, nor of him who runs, but of God who shows mercy. ¹⁷ For the Scripture says to the Pharaoh, "For this very purpose I have raised you up, that I may show My power in you, and that My name may be declared in all the earth." ¹⁸ Therefore He has mercy on whom He wills, and whom He wills He hardens.

¹⁹ You will say to me then, "Why does He still find fault? For who has resisted His will?" ²⁰ But indeed, O man, who are you to reply against God? Will the thing formed say to him who formed it, "Why have you made me like this?" ²¹ Does not the potter have power over the clay, from the same lump to make one vessel for honor and another for dishonor?

3. God had chosen the Israelites (represented by Jacob) for His divine purposes, but the fact that He did not chose other peoples (represented by Esau) does not mean that He is a God of injustice. What does Paul say about God's sovereignty in this regard (see verses 14–18)?

_____

_____

_____

_____

_____

4. What objection does Paul anticipate that his opponents will raise (see verse 19)? What is Paul's immediate response to this argument (see verses 20–21)?

_____

_____

_____

_____

God's Supreme Sovereignty (Romans 9:22–29)

22 What if God, wanting to show His wrath and to make His power known, endured with much longsuffering the vessels of wrath prepared for destruction, 23 and that He might make known the riches of His glory on the vessels of mercy, which He had prepared beforehand for glory, 24 even us whom He called, not of the Jews only, but also of the Gentiles?

25 As He says also in Hosea:

"I will call them My people, who were not My people,
And her beloved, who was not beloved."

²⁶ "And it shall come to pass in the place where it was said
  to them,
'You are not My people,'
There they shall be called sons of the living God."

²⁷ Isaiah also cries out concerning Israel:

"Though the number of the children of Israel be as the sand of
  the sea,
The remnant will be saved.
²⁸ For He will finish the work and cut it short in righteousness,
Because the LORD will make a short work upon the earth."

²⁹ And as Isaiah said before:

"Unless the LORD of Sabaoth had left us a seed,
We would have become like Sodom,
And we would have been made like Gomorrah."

---

5. Paul's point in this section is that those who receive salvation do so only through the mercy of God, while those who do not receive salvation do so by their rejection of God's mercy. Given this, who represents the "vessels of wrath prepared for destruction" (verse 22)?

6. How do the passages that Paul cites from the Old Testament reveal that God's purposes extend to more than just members of the Jewish race (see verses 25–29)?

_____

_____

_____

_____

_____

_____

Israel's Continued Unbelief (Romans 9:30–33)

³⁰ What shall we say then? That Gentiles, who did not pursue righteousness, have attained to righteousness, even the righteousness of faith; ³¹ but Israel, pursuing the law of righteousness, has not attained to the law of righteousness. ³² Why? Because they did not seek it by faith, but as it were, by the works of the law. For they stumbled at that stumbling stone. ³³ As it is written:

> "Behold, I lay in Zion a stumbling stone and rock of offense,
> And whoever believes on Him will not be put to shame."

7. Spiritually speaking, what made the Gentiles different from the Jews (see verse 30)?

_____

_____

_____

_____

_____

_____

8. How does Paul figuratively describe what happened to the Jews when they sought righteousness through the works of the law (see verses 32–33)?

_____

_____

_____

_____

_____

_____

REVIEWING THE STORY

In this section, Paul addresses a spiritual dilemma regarding the nation of Israel—God's chosen people who had sadly chosen to reject Jesus as their promised Messiah. The question Paul raises is whether this indicates God's plan for His people had failed and, if so, what that means for His plans for us. But Paul is quick to point out that Israel's rejection of the Messiah did not take God by surprise. God is all-powerful _and_ all-knowing, and He knew that some would reject the gospel. This does not make God unfair or unrighteous—in fact, _no one_ would be saved if it were not for God's mercy. Of course, the fact that God is sovereign and knows all does not negate our own responsibility. We must choose to accept Christ and follow after Him.

9. What are some of the blessings the people of Israel received from God (see Romans 9:4)?

_____

_____

_____

_____

_____

10. What does it mean that "not all Israel . . . are of Israel" (see Romans 9:9)?

_____

_____

_____

_____

_____

_____

_____

11. How did God explain to Moses His criteria for showing mercy (see Romans 9:15)?

_____

_____

_____

_____

_____

_____

_____

12. Why did the people of Israel, who pursued the law of righteousness, not attain the law of righteousness (see Romans 9:32)?

_____

_____

_____

_____

_____

_____

_____

APPLYING THE MESSAGE

13. Paul felt deep anguish that his own people had not embraced the message of Christ. Who are some people in your life whom you pray would come to know the gospel?

---

14. People in Paul's day questioned if God had "failed" in His plans for Israel. What causes people today to doubt that God always has a purpose and always is in control?

REFLECTING ON THE MEANING

In this section of Paul's letter to the believers in Rome, we discover that God's plan to save humanity was realized through the death and resurrection of Jesus Christ. As Paul writes in Romans 9:32–33:

> For they [the people of Israel] stumbled at that stumbling stone.
> As it is written: "Behold, I lay in Zion a stumbling stone and rock
> of offense, and whoever believes on Him will not be put to shame."

If you study the Bible, you will discover this reference has to do with the crucified Christ. The stumbling stone is Jesus. In 1 Corinthians 1:23, Paul puts it this way: "But we preach Christ crucified, to the Jews a stumbling block and to the Greeks foolishness." The Jewish people had stumbled at the crucified Savior for the same reason people stumble today. The crucified Savior undermines our own self-righteousness. The fact that Christ died for our sins is proof positive that we cannot save ourselves. To make this confession is an intolerable offense to our pride. So, instead of humbling ourselves, we stumble over the stumbling stone.

Often times, when those who have not accepted the message of Christ are asked how they expect to get into heaven, they respond by saying, "I try to live a good life," or, "I come from a good family and I've never done anything really bad," or, "I go to church, and I'm a good, upstanding citizen in my community." They believe that because they have *tried* to live well, that will somehow earn them a pass for their sins and get them into eternity. If you inform them that they are lost *because* of their sin, it's usually the end of the conversation. They cannot comprehend the gospel—who Christ is and what He did for them.

In truth, it is difficult for all of us to deal with the fact we cannot save ourselves. But it's the *truth*. People stumble over the truth about Jesus. The Jews did it in Paul's day, and they do it today. We have to realize our own moral bankruptcy before we're willing to come to Christ. We have to accept the fact that what we want, He has—and He's the only One who has it.

JOURNALING YOUR RESPONSE

How can you help people avoid stumbling over the truth of Christ?

GOD'S PLAN OF RIGHTEOUSNESS

Romans 10:1–21

GETTING STARTED

Why do you think that some people become hardened to the message of the gospel?

SETTING THE STAGE

Paul has now addressed the doctrine of God's sovereignty and raised the question as to whether or not God is just. The apostle's conclusion is that God is the sovereign Creator and Ruler over all, and we have no right to question the One who has made us. God has the right to do with us as He pleases. It is completely within His perfect and sovereign will as to whom He chooses to extend mercy and to whom He relegates tasks for His service.

But if we stopped our study of Romans at this point, we would be left with just enough vertical theology to make us horizontally irresponsible. We could make an argument that God's sovereignty means we don't need to present the gospel of Christ to the lost. We could say, "Well, if God chooses a person, then it doesn't really matter what they do. God will save them or not . . . I have no part in that outcome." Likewise, we could make the argument that it does not matter what *we* do personally. We could say, "It doesn't really matter if I follow God's commands. If God has chosen me, God will save me. I don't have to do anything about it."

However, Paul makes it clear that while God is in control, He also makes us *responsible*. We cannot enter the mind of God. We don't know why God chooses to call and use some individuals and not others. He is the One who makes the choice . . . and He doesn't bring us into His decision-making process. So, our responsibility as God's people is to pray and to go into all the world to preach the gospel. We are to live as if the entire matter was up to us—all the while remembering that we serve a sovereign God who alone is in charge.

EXPLORING THE TEXT

Israel Needs the Gospel (Romans 10:1–4)

[1] Brethren, my heart's desire and prayer to God for Israel is that they may be saved. [2] For I bear them witness that they have a zeal for God, but not according to knowledge. [3] For they being ignorant of God's

righteousness, and seeking to establish their own righteousness, have not submitted to the righteousness of God. ⁴ For Christ is the end of the law for righteousness to everyone who believes.

---

1. Paul has spoken about Israel's failure to accept Jesus as their Messiah. However, he understood their plight because he once shared the same attitude concerning Christ. What is Paul's desire for them (see verse 1)?

_____

_____

_____

_____

_____

_____

2. What does Paul identify as the primary cause of this refusal (see verses 2–4)?

_____

_____

_____

_____

_____

_____

_____

Confess and Believe (Romans 10:5–13)

⁵ For Moses writes about the righteousness which is of the law, "The man who does those things shall live by them." ⁶ But the righteousness of faith speaks in this way, "Do not say in your heart, 'Who will ascend into heaven?' " (that is, to bring Christ down from above) ⁷ or, " 'Who

will descend into the abyss?' " (that is, to bring Christ up from the dead). ⁸ But what does it say? "The word is near you, in your mouth and in your heart" (that is, the word of faith which we preach): ⁹ that if you confess with your mouth the Lord Jesus and believe in your heart that God has raised Him from the dead, you will be saved. ¹⁰ For with the heart one believes unto righteousness, and with the mouth confession is made unto salvation. ¹¹ For the Scripture says, "Whoever believes on Him will not be put to shame." ¹² For there is no distinction between Jew and Greek, for the same Lord over all is rich to all who call upon Him. ¹³ For "whoever calls on the name of the Lᴏʀᴅ shall be saved."

---

3. What does Paul state that Moses wrote about the law? How does a person attain righteousness according to the Law of Moses (see verse 5)?

_____

_____

_____

_____

_____

4. Paul quotes Moses as saying, "The word is very near you, in your mouth and in your heart" (see Deuteronomy 30:14), to show that salvation is a matter of *confessing* (your mouth) and *believing* (your heart). How does Paul expand on this point (see verses 8–13)?

_____

_____

_____

_____

_____

_____

The Believer's Role (Romans 10:14–17)

¹⁴ How then shall they call on Him in whom they have not believed? And how shall they believe in Him of whom they have not heard? And how shall they hear without a preacher? ¹⁵ And how shall they preach unless they are sent? As it is written:

> "How beautiful are the feet of those who preach the gospel of
> peace,
> Who bring glad tidings of good things!"

¹⁶ But they have not all obeyed the gospel. For Isaiah says, "LORD, who has believed our report?" ¹⁷ So then faith comes by hearing, and hearing by the word of God.

5. Paul now turns to the importance of proclaiming the gospel of Christ to the lost. What call does he give to his fellow believers at this point (see verses 14–15)?

6. According to Paul, how does a person come to faith in God (see verses 16–17)?

Israel Rejects the Gospel (Romans 10:18–21)

¹⁸ But I say, have they not heard? Yes indeed:

"Their sound has gone out to all the earth,
And their words to the ends of the world."

¹⁹ But I say, did Israel not know? First Moses says:

"I will provoke you to jealousy by those who are not a nation,
I will move you to anger by a foolish nation."

²⁰ But Isaiah is very bold and says:

"I was found by those who did not seek Me;
I was made manifest to those who did not ask for Me."

²¹ But to Israel he says:

"All day long I have stretched out My hands
To a disobedient and contrary people."

7. Paul first quotes from Psalm 19:4 and Deuteronomy 32:21. How do these passages answer his question as to whether Israel had heard the gospel (see Romans 10:18–19)?

_____

_____

_____

_____

_____

_____

8. Paul next quotes from Isaiah 65:1–2. What did God do after His people rejected the gospel? What is God continually attempting to do (see Romans 10:20–21)?

_____

_____

_____

_____

_____

_____

REVIEWING THE STORY

Paul expressed his heart's desire that Israel would channel its misguided zeal for God into an understanding that Jesus was their promised Messiah. He desired for them to turn away from their efforts to establish their own righteousness by the law and look to their own Scriptures for the knowledge that would lead them to find true salvation in Christ. He emphasized that righteousness comes from confessing that Jesus Christ is Lord and believing that God raised Him from the dead. Paul then focuses on the necessity of preaching the gospel, though he acknowledges—using the testimony of David, Moses, and Isaiah—that not everyone who hears the gospel of Christ will be open to receive that gospel in their hearts.

9. What mistake did the Israelites make in their zeal for God (see Romans 10:2–3)?

_____

_____

_____

_____

_____

10. What does a person have to do in order to be saved
(see Romans 10:9)?

11. From where do faith and hearing the gospel originate
(see Romans 10:17)?

12. How does God describe those of His chosen people who refuse
Christ (see Romans 10:21)?

APPLYING THE MESSAGE

13. Paul notes the Israelites who rejected Christ had a zeal for God but
not according to knowledge (see Romans 10:2). Why is misguided zeal
such a problem?

14. Paul writes, "How shall [the lost] hear without a preacher?" (verse 14). Who comes to mind when you read this? What action do you sense God is asking you to take?

_____

_____

_____

_____

REFLECTING ON THE MEANING

In this section, Paul writes a simple formula for salvation: "If you confess with your mouth the Lord Jesus and believe in your heart that God has raised Him from the dead, you will be saved" (Romans 10:9). His words reveal it is necessary to *confess* Christ just as it is necessary to have *faith* in Him. Some people fall into the trap of living as "secret" Christians. They have believed in Christ, but they don't want anybody else to know about it. Maybe they are afraid that such an outward confession would hurt their business or relationships. Maybe they just want to blend in with their peers. Maybe they are afraid people will expect them to act differently.

But the reality is there are no secret Christians. If you are truly saved—if you believe with your heart, mind, emotions, and will that Jesus is Lord—your mouth will never be totally quiet about it. Your faith will interrupt your life. You will be compelled to bring it up and talk about it at the most inconvenient moments. It is going to show up when you least expect it. Why? Because it is the natural result of who you are.

You may say, "I'm just a quiet person," or, "I don't have the gift of evangelism." While those statements may be true, remember there are many ways to confess Christ. You confess Him first with baptism. You confess Him in your church attendance. You confess Him in the outward testimony of your life. You confess Him in the way you do business. You confess Him by your public allegiance to Him and your unwillingness to be ashamed of Him.

When you receive God's gift of salvation, old things pass away and all things become new. You are changed, and you start talking about what has happened in your life. In a practical way, you start *confessing* Christ.

JOURNALING YOUR RESPONSE

What are some of the ways that you confess Christ each and every day?

THE DESTINY OF ISRAEL

Romans 11:1–36

GETTING STARTED

How would you react if someone you love continually rejected you?

_____

_____

_____

_____

_____

_____

_____

_____

_____

_____

_____

_____

_____

_____

_____

_____

_____

_____

SETTING THE STAGE

Paul has painted a rather bleak picture of Israel's response to the gospel. But in this next section, he reminds his readers that God has not forgotten His people. While some today may believe that God no longer has a purpose for Israel or the Jewish people, Paul's words in these passages remind us that God has an unfailing and unconditional love for the people of Israel.

As we have seen, Paul's focus in this section is on how to harmonize the Jewish people's refusal of their Messiah with the covenants of God that were given to them—which said they would ultimately believe. Paul first presented the argument that God is sovereign and can do whatever He pleases, but it pleases Him to express His sovereignty in mercy toward those who believe (see Romans 9). He added that people are not lost because God desires for them to be lost, but because they choose to be lost (see Romans 10).

In this section, Paul will continue to develop his arguments by addressing an issue many people were discussing in his day: "Has God cast away His people"? Paul's answer to this question is an emphatic, "Certainly not!" (11:1). Paul believed that God always had a plan for Israel in the past and *still* had a plan for His people in the future—even though they have rejected their Messiah. While the focus of the gospel efforts might have shifted to the Gentiles, God had not forgotten his people and had not rejected them.

The promise of Scripture is that God is going to do a marvelous work on behalf of the Jewish people. He is not through with them. As Paul states, "Now if their fall is riches for the world, and their failure riches for the Gentiles, how much more their fullness!" (Romans 11:12).

EXPLORING THE TEXT

A Remnant in Israel (Romans 11:1–6)

¹ I say then, has God cast away His people? Certainly not! For I also am an Israelite, of the seed of Abraham, of the tribe of Benjamin.
² God has not cast away His people whom He foreknew. Or do you

not know what the Scripture says of Elijah, how he pleads with God against Israel, saying, ³ "LORD, they have killed Your prophets and torn down Your altars, and I alone am left, and they seek my life"? ⁴ But what does the divine response say to him? "I have reserved for Myself seven thousand men who have not bowed the knee to Baal." ⁵ Even so then, at this present time there is a remnant according to the election of grace. ⁶ And if by grace, then it is no longer of works; otherwise grace is no longer grace. But if it is of works, it is no longer grace; otherwise work is no longer work.

---

1. So far, Paul has stressed God's sovereignty in choosing Israel and His response to Israel's rejection of the Messiah. But still the issue remains: how do we reconcile the fact that God *chose* the Israelites for His plan of salvation but they *chose* to reject that plan? What evidence does Paul offer that God *still* has a plan for them (see verses 1–3)?

_____

_____

_____

_____

_____

_____

2. The prophet Elijah had despaired that he was the only one left who served the Lord, but God revealed He had reserved a remnant who still followed Him (see 1 Kings 19:14–18). How does Paul apply this example to the people of Israel in his day (see Romans 11:4–6)?

_____

_____

_____

_____

_____

Not Seeing or Hearing (Romans 11:7–12)

⁷ What then? Israel has not obtained what it seeks; but the elect have obtained it, and the rest were blinded. ⁸ Just as it is written:

"God has given them a spirit of stupor,
Eyes that they should not see
And ears that they should not hear,
To this very day."

⁹ And David says:

"Let their table become a snare and a trap,
A stumbling block and a recompense to them.
¹⁰ Let their eyes be darkened, so that they do not see,
And bow down their back always."

¹¹ I say then, have they stumbled that they should fall? Certainly not! But through their fall, to provoke them to jealousy, salvation has come to the Gentiles. ¹² Now if their fall is riches for the world, and their failure riches for the Gentiles, how much more their fullness!

3. Paul's first quote is from Deuteronomy 29:4 and Isaiah 29:10. The people of Israel were "blind" to what God was doing when He delivered them from Egypt and "deaf" to the prophets He sent with warnings to repent. How does Paul imply that this same attitude has carried over to the Jewish people of his day (see Romans 11:7–8)?

4. Paul's second quote is from Psalm 69:22–23, which he applies to the Israelites who have rejected Jesus. But what hope does Paul provide for them (see Romans 11:9–12)?

Ingrafted Branches (Romans 11:13–24)

13 For I speak to you Gentiles; inasmuch as I am an apostle to the Gentiles, I magnify my ministry, 14 if by any means I may provoke to jealousy those who are my flesh and save some of them. 15 For if their being cast away is the reconciling of the world, what will their acceptance be but life from the dead?

16 For if the firstfruit is holy, the lump is also holy; and if the root is holy, so are the branches. 17 And if some of the branches were broken off, and you, being a wild olive tree, were grafted in among them, and with them became a partaker of the root and fatness of the olive tree, 18 do not boast against the branches. But if you do boast, remember that you do not support the root, but the root supports you.

19 You will say then, "Branches were broken off that I might be grafted in." 20 Well said. Because of unbelief they were broken off, and you stand by faith. Do not be haughty, but fear. 21 For if God did not spare the natural branches, He may not spare you either. 22 Therefore consider the goodness and severity of God: on those who fell, severity; but toward you, goodness, if you continue in His

goodness. Otherwise you also will be cut off. ²³ And they also, if they do not continue in unbelief, will be grafted in, for God is able to graft them in again. ²⁴ For if you were cut out of the olive tree which is wild by nature, and were grafted contrary to nature into a cultivated olive tree, how much more will these, who are natural branches, be grafted into their own olive tree?

---

5. Paul is known to his readers as the "apostle of the Gentiles," but he wants them to know he is deeply concerned about the Jewish people's need for the gospel. What does Paul say the Jews' rejection of the gospel will actually bring (see verses 13–16)?

_____

_____

_____

_____

_____

_____

6. The Gentiles were "grafted in" to God's greater plan that began with the Jewish race. How does Paul say they should now act? What warning does he give to them (see verses 19–22)?

_____

_____

_____

_____

_____

_____

_____

All Israel Will Be Saved (Romans 11:25–36)

²⁵ For I do not desire, brethren, that you should be ignorant of this mystery, lest you should be wise in your own opinion, that blindness in part has happened to Israel until the fullness of the Gentiles has come in. ²⁶ And so all Israel will be saved, as it is written:

> "The Deliverer will come out of Zion,
> And He will turn away ungodliness
>   from Jacob;
> ²⁷ For this is My covenant with them,
> When I take away their sins."

²⁸ Concerning the gospel they are enemies for your sake, but concerning the election they are beloved for the sake of the fathers. ²⁹ For the gifts and the calling of God are irrevocable. ³⁰ For as you were once disobedient to God, yet have now obtained mercy through their disobedience, ³¹ even so these also have now been disobedient, that through the mercy shown you they also may obtain mercy. ³² For God has committed them all to disobedience, that He might have mercy on all.

³³ Oh, the depth of the riches both of the wisdom and knowledge of God! How unsearchable are His judgments and His ways past finding out!

> ³⁴ "For who has known the mind of the Lord?
> Or who has become His counselor?"
> ³⁵ "Or who has first given to Him
> And it shall be repaid to him?"

³⁶ For of Him and through Him and to Him are all things, to whom be glory forever. Amen.

7. Paul opens this passage by speaking of a "mystery," which refers to God's actions with His people in the past that are now being revealed in the present. What is this mystery to which Paul refers? What does Paul say about the fate of Israel (see verses 25–27)?

_____

_____

_____

_____

_____

8. What paradox does Paul mention concerning the Jews and the Gentiles (see verses 28–32)? How does Paul conclude this narrative on the mysteries of God (see verses 33–36)?

_____

_____

_____

_____

_____

_____

_____

REVIEWING THE STORY

Paul offered hope for the Jewish race by pointing out that God has not cast away His people. Throughout Israel's history (most notably during the time of Elijah), God had worked with a faithful remnant after the majority of His people had rejected Him. According to His grace, God had allowed some Israelites to recognize the truth of the gospel and left others to be blind to it. He allowed Israel to stumble so the Gentiles could receive the gospel. But Paul did not want the Gentiles to feel superior about their status. Rather, they had been grafted into a tree whose roots were Jewish. One day, those in Israel who rejected Jesus as the Messiah will come to understand the truth of the gospel and in this way will be saved.

9. In Paul's retelling of Elijah's story, how did the Lord reply when Elijah pointed out that Israel had rejected Him and killed His prophets (see Romans 11:3–4)?

_____

_____

_____

_____

_____

10. What is the difference between the "elect" and the "non-elect"? What reasons does Paul provide for the non-elect not receiving the gospel (see Romans 11:7–8)?

_____

_____

_____

_____

_____

11. How did Paul say the Gentiles were to view the fact they had been "grafted in" to God's plan of salvation (see Romans 11:19–22)?

_____

_____

_____

_____

_____

12. How long will the spiritual blindness of Israel continue (see Romans 11:25)?

_____

_____

_____

_____

_____

APPLYING THE MESSAGE

13. Why do you think people reject the message of Christ today?

_____

_____

_____

_____

_____

14. How can you, as someone who has embraced the gospel, present it to others in a way that resonates with them?

_____

_____

_____

_____

_____

REFLECTING ON THE MEANING

There are few passages in the Bible more difficult to understand than Paul's words in this chapter of Romans. Yet there are also few passages in the Bible that tell us more about God and His promises than this chapter of the Bible. As we reflect on Paul's words, there are four main takeaways we should consider.

First, *God's promises are unfailing*. God made unconditional promises to Israel through their history. More often than not, Israel responded to these promises with indifference and, ultimately, with outward rebellion that resulted in the crucifixion of the Messiah. They put the One whom God had sent on a cross and killed Him. Yet God did not—and *will not*—go back on His promise to His people. His promises can be trusted. He will do what He said He will do. Whether we do everything we should do or not, God's promises will not fail.

Second, *God's providence is unfathomable*. God does His work in strange ways. Who would have thought the Gentiles would come to faith in Christ by way of the rejection of the Messiah by the Jews? God's providence is beyond our comprehension. Paul states, "We know that all things work together for good to those who love God" (Romans 8:28). When we see how the plan of redemption unfolds across the panorama of history, we realize that God is at work even in things that sometimes look to us like failures.

Third, *God's purpose is unchangeable*. Despite all the Israelites did to defeat and thwart God's purpose, they discovered that He will not and cannot be denied. He will always ultimately accomplish what He originally set out to accomplish. The apostle Paul himself could only marvel that God had chosen to use him—a "Hebrew of the Hebrews" (Philippians 3:5) and the "worst" of sinners (see 1 Timothy 1:15)—to bring about the spread of the gospel to the Gentiles. As the psalmist wrote, "Whatever the LORD pleases He does, in heaven and in earth" (Psalm 135:6).

Fourth, *God's power is undisputed*. God's purposes can—and *will*—overrule all the evil devices of people. The Lord takes that which people mean for evil and turns it into good. Joseph discovered as much when he reflected on everything he had endured in his life and declared to his brothers, "You meant evil against me; but God meant it for good, in order to bring it about as it is this day, to save many people alive" (Genesis 50:20). God can use anything to accomplish His will. No matter how we fight Him or struggle against Him, God's will always prevails.

JOURNALING YOUR RESPONSE

When have you seen God work through unexpected people or circumstances to accomplish His purpose and will in your life?

RENEWED MINDS

Romans 12:1–21

GETTING STARTED

When you think of the body of Christ, what part do you see yourself in that body? Why?

Setting the Stage

As you look at the structure of Romans, you discover that chapters 1–8 teach the *principles* of the gospel, chapters 9–11 deal with the *problems* of the gospel, and chapters 12–16 deal with the *practice* of the gospel. It is in this final section, chapters 12–16, where you take the truth Paul has taught and make it work in your life. Paul begins this final section with this summary statement:

> I beseech you therefore, brethren, by the mercies of God, that you present your bodies a living sacrifice, holy, acceptable to God, which is your reasonable service. And do not be conformed to this world, but be transformed by the renewing of your mind, that you may prove what is that good and acceptable and perfect will of God" (verses 1–2).

Notice that Paul writes in the *present* tense: "Do not be conformed to this world, but *be transformed*" (emphasis added). This means the transformation is a continual process. You don't just undergo transformation in an instant and then stay that way indefinitely. You continue to be transformed again and again. It's a daily process.

Furthermore, Paul writes not only in the present tense but also in the *passive voice*. This means the subject doesn't *take* the action; the action is *on* the subject. You cannot transform your own mind—only the Holy Spirit can. But you must make yourself available to the Holy Spirit so He can renew your mind. You do this through Scripture—by getting into the Word of God on a daily basis. Whether it's taught, listened to, read, memorized, or understood, the Word of God is the material the Holy Spirit uses to transform you and renew your mind.

Finally, Paul writes not only in the present tense and the passive voice but also in the *imperative mood*. The imperative mood is a command. While you cannot renew your own mind, you still have responsibilities you must fulfill in the process. You are commanded to allow this transformation to occur in your life—to cooperate with the Holy Spirit to the fullest.

EXPLORING THE TEXT

Living Sacrifices to God (Romans 12:1–2)

> ¹ I beseech you therefore, brethren, by the mercies of God, that you present your bodies a living sacrifice, holy, acceptable to God, which is your reasonable service. ² And do not be conformed to this world, but be transformed by the renewing of your mind, that you may prove what is that good and acceptable and perfect will of God.

1. Now that Paul has outlined what *God* has done in terms of the gospel, he will outline what *believers* are expected to do in response to the gospel. What is the first point that Paul mentions? What do you think he means by "living sacrifice" (see verse 1)?

_____

_____

_____

_____

_____

2. What must believers do instead of being conformed to this world (see verse 2)?

_____

_____

_____

_____

_____

_____

_____

Service in the Body of Christ (Romans 12:3–8)

³ For I say, through the grace given to me, to everyone who is among you, not to think of himself more highly than he ought to think, but to think soberly, as God has dealt to each one a measure of faith. ⁴ For as we have many members in one body, but all the members do not have the same function, ⁵ so we, being many, are one body in Christ, and individually members of one another. ⁶ Having then gifts differing according to the grace that is given to us, let us use them: if prophecy, let us prophesy in proportion to our faith; ⁷ or ministry, let us use it in our ministering; he who teaches, in teaching; ⁸ he who exhorts, in exhortation; he who gives, with liberality; he who leads, with diligence; he who shows mercy, with cheerfulness.

3. Paul recognizes that different people in the body of Christ will possess different gifts, which could become an issue of pride for some and envy for others. What counsel does he provide to combat these types of attitudes from forming in the church (see verse 3)?

4. How does the church function like a human body? Why is it so critical that all of the parts—with their different roles—function to serve the whole (see verses 4–8)?

_____

_____

_____

_____

_____

Love in Action (Romans 12:9–16)

⁹ Let love be without hypocrisy. Abhor what is evil. Cling to what is good. ¹⁰ Be kindly affectionate to one another with brotherly love, in honor giving preference to one another; ¹¹ not lagging in diligence, fervent in spirit, serving the Lord; ¹² rejoicing in hope, patient in tribulation, continuing steadfastly in prayer; ¹³ distributing to the needs of the saints, given to hospitality.

¹⁴ Bless those who persecute you; bless and do not curse. ¹⁵ Rejoice with those who rejoice, and weep with those who weep. ¹⁶ Be of the same mind toward one another. Do not set your mind on high things, but associate with the humble. Do not be wise in your own opinion.

5. In this section, Paul draws on sayings of Jesus (known through oral tradition) that eventually appear as part of the Sermon on the Mount in Matthew's Gospel. What behaviors and attitudes are necessary for the church to function as God intends (see verses 10–13)?

_____

_____

_____

_____

_____

6. Paul comments not only on how believers are to act with one another but also with the outside world. How does he say believers are to respond when faced with persecution and trials? How should they treat others and think of themselves (see verses 14–16)?

_____

_____

_____

_____

Behaving Like a Christian (Romans 12:17–21)

[17] Repay no one evil for evil. Have regard for good things in the sight of all men. [18] If it is possible, as much as depends on you, live peaceably with all men. [19] Beloved, do not avenge yourselves, but rather give place to wrath; for it is written, "Vengeance is Mine, I will repay," says the Lord. [20] Therefore

"If your enemy is hungry, feed him;
If he is thirsty, give him a drink;
For in so doing you will heap coals of fire on his head."

[21] Do not be overcome by evil, but overcome evil with good.

7. Why is it critical to not repay evil for evil when it comes to the mission of a believer in Christ? Why do you think it is important to live peaceably with others (see verses 17–18)?

_____

_____

_____

_____

8. What should believers do when they feel the need to get revenge on someone? What promise do they have from God in this regard (see verses 19–21)?

REVIEWING THE STORY

Paul offers believers in this section of the letter a basic primer in Christian living. His words encourage us to present ourselves as sacrifices to God— vessels fit for His work. This involves resisting the influence of this world and learning to think differently. It involves putting to use the gifts that God has given us and working in unity with other uniquely gifted believers. It involves behaving with those outside the church in such a way that they recognize Christ in us. It involves showing love to those who oppose us, interacting with others in an empathetic and service-oriented way, and maintaining a humble spirit.

9. Why must we be transformed by the renewing of our minds (see Romans 12:2)?

10. What spiritual gifts does Paul single out in his exhortation to the Roman believers (see Romans 12:6–8)?

11. What should your response be to those who persecute you (see Romans 12:14)?

_____

_____

_____

_____

_____

_____

12. What does Paul say that you should do for your enemies (see Romans 12:20)?

_____

_____

_____

_____

_____

_____

APPLYING THE MESSAGE

13. In what areas of your life do you struggle with being conformed to this world?

_____

_____

_____

_____

_____

14. What are some ways that you could make better use of your spiritual gifts?

Reflecting on the Meaning

Paul urged his readers to behave like followers of Jesus and present themselves as "a living sacrifice, holy, acceptable to God" (12:1). This, Paul wrote, could be accomplished by allowing the Holy Spirit to renew their minds, by serving their brothers and sisters within the body of Christ, by loving other people without hypocrisy, and by not taking vengeance on others.

Paul ends this portion of his letter by reminding you to show kindness—rather than evil—to those who wrong you. Suppose a sister in Christ says something hurtful to you, and you retaliate by saying something mean to her. In order for her to stay in the game, she has to think of something meaner than what you said and say it back to you. As the encounter progresses, the stakes get higher. Before you know it, awful things are being said.

How does the cycle stop? When one of you decides to be big enough, strong enough, and Spirit-filled enough to say, "I am going to hand this over to God and choose not to retaliate." You counter the other person's hurtful words with a sincere compliment, gracious invitation, or heartfelt apology. You give back something undeserved and, in the process, change an enemy into a friend. This is the *only* way to stop the cycle of hurt. If you wait to get the last word, you will be in the cycle for the rest of your life.

As with all things godly, the Lord Jesus is our example. He was bitterly abused and mistreated, yet He answered not a word. He was taken as a lamb to the slaughter, yet He said not a word. He could have called ten thousand angels, but He didn't ask for help. He took the worst that people could throw at Him and absorbed it all. The result is that we have been set free from our sin. This freedom allows us to love other people—even our enemies.

JOURNALING YOUR RESPONSE

What steps can you take to break a cycle of retaliation—and make a friend of an enemy?

SUBJECT TO AUTHORITY

Romans 13:1–14:23

GETTING STARTED

Why is it so harmful for Christians to judge one another?

SETTING THE STAGE

In this next section of Romans, the apostle Paul sets forth one of the most notables passages in the New Testament on how a believer should respond to human authority. It is possible that Paul's primary readers, being based in the capital of the Roman Empire, had become hostile to the government after the Emperor Claudius expelled all Christians from Rome (see Acts 18:2). It is also quite likely that many had questions as to how far they should submit to Roman rule. After all, if God is the ultimate authority, why should they submit to human authority?

Paul's response is based on the teachings of Jesus on the subject. During Christ's time on earth, His enemies would often try to trap Him with questions designed to back Him into a corner. On one occasion, a group of Pharisees (the Jewish religious elite) and Herodians (a group loyal to the government) attempted to trap Jesus with a carefully worded question: "Teacher, we know that You are true, and teach the way of God in truth. . . . Tell us, therefore, what do You think? Is it lawful to pay taxes to Caesar, or not?" (Matthew 22:16–17).

These two groups knew that if Jesus said the Jewish people should *not* pay taxes to Caesar, then He could be branded as a traitor to the Roman government. On the other hand, if Jesus said that the people *should* pay taxes to Caesar, He could be viewed as the enemy of His own people and lose credibility with them. As far as the inquisitors were concerned, there was no way out for the Lord. Of course, they greatly underestimated Him.

Matthew relates what happened next: "Jesus perceived their wickedness, and said, 'Why do you test Me, you hypocrites? Show Me the tax money.' So they brought Him a denarius. And He said to them, 'Whose image and inscription is this?' They said to Him, 'Caesar's'" (Matthew 22:18–21). Jesus' next statement stopped them in their tracks: "Render therefore to Caesar the things that are Caesar's, and to God the things that are God's" (verse 21). When His opponents heard these words, they marveled at Him and went their way.

This interchange reveals that Jesus affirmed the validity of human government—for God had been the One to establish it as an institution on the earth. Yet in His brief answer, He also set limits on human government: the things that belong to Caesar are to be given to him, and the things that belong to God are to be given to Him. Paul will take this very same position—agreeing that we are to submit to God *first* and then to the human authorities He has established.

EXPLORING THE TEXT

Submit to Government (Romans 13:1–7)

> [1] Let every soul be subject to the governing authorities. For there is no authority except from God, and the authorities that exist are appointed by God. [2] Therefore whoever resists the authority resists the ordinance of God, and those who resist will bring judgment on themselves. [3] For rulers are not a terror to good works, but to evil. Do you want to be unafraid of the authority? Do what is good, and you will have praise from the same. [4] For he is God's minister to you for good. But if you do evil, be afraid; for he does not bear the sword in vain; for he is God's minister, an avenger to execute wrath on him who practices evil. [5] Therefore you must be subject, not only because of wrath but also for conscience' sake. [6] For because of this you also pay taxes, for they are God's ministers attending continually to this very thing. [7] Render therefore to all their due: taxes to whom taxes are due, customs to whom customs, fear to whom fear, honor to whom honor.

1. Paul recognized that a believer's citizenship was ultimately in heaven (see Philippians 3:20), but he is clear this reality did not excuse anyone from his or her responsibilities as a citizen of a city, state, or country.

What does Paul say about human authority in this passage? Why should believers submit to their governing authorities (see Romans 13:1–3)?

2. In what ways does human government act as "God's minister" on earth? Why did Paul say it was proper for believers in Christ to thus pay taxes to their government (see verses 4–7)?

Love Your Neighbor (Romans 13:8–14)

⁸ Owe no one anything except to love one another, for he who loves another has fulfilled the law. ⁹ For the commandments, "You shall not commit adultery," "You shall not murder," "You shall not steal," "You shall not bear false witness," "You shall not covet," and if there is any other commandment, are all summed up in this saying, namely, "You shall love your neighbor as yourself." ¹⁰ Love does no harm to a neighbor; therefore love is the fulfillment of the law.

¹¹ And do this, knowing the time, that now it is high time to awake out of sleep; for now our salvation is nearer than when we first

believed. [12] The night is far spent, the day is at hand. Therefore let us cast off the works of darkness, and let us put on the armor of light. [13] Let us walk properly, as in the day, not in revelry and drunkenness, not in lewdness and lust, not in strife and envy. [14] But put on the Lord Jesus Christ, and make no provision for the flesh, to fulfill its lusts.

---

3. Paul has just stated that believers should pay taxes to all in government who are owed such amounts. But when it comes to the body of Christ, the believers are to owe *nothing* to one another . . . except love. Why do you think Paul makes this statement? Why is it acceptable for believers in Christ to only owe love to each other (see verses 8–10)?

_____

_____

_____

_____

_____

_____

4. What does Paul mean when he says that we should "awake out of sleep"? What is required to "walk properly" with the Lord each day (see verses 11–14)?

_____

_____

_____

_____

_____

_____

_____

The Law of Liberty (Romans 14:1–13)

¹ Receive one who is weak in the faith, but not to disputes over doubtful things. ² For one believes he may eat all things, but he who is weak eats only vegetables. ³ Let not him who eats despise him who does not eat, and let not him who does not eat judge him who eats; for God has received him. ⁴ Who are you to judge another's servant? To his own master he stands or falls. Indeed, he will be made to stand, for God is able to make him stand.

⁵ One person esteems one day above another; another esteems every day alike. Let each be fully convinced in his own mind. ⁶ He who observes the day, observes it to the Lord; and he who does not observe the day, to the Lord he does not observe it. He who eats, eats to the Lord, for he gives God thanks; and he who does not eat, to the Lord he does not eat, and gives God thanks. ⁷ For none of us lives to himself, and no one dies to himself. ⁸ For if we live, we live to the Lord; and if we die, we die to the Lord. Therefore, whether we live or die, we are the Lord's. ⁹ For to this end Christ died and rose and lived again, that He might be Lord of both the dead and the living. ¹⁰ But why do you judge your brother? Or why do you show contempt for your brother? For we shall all stand before the judgment seat of Christ. ¹¹ For it is written:

> "As I live, says the LORD,
> Every knee shall bow to Me,
> And every tongue shall confess to God."

¹² So then each of us shall give account of himself to God. ¹³ Therefore let us not judge one another anymore, but rather resolve this, not to put a stumbling block or a cause to fall in our brother's way.

5. Paul's instruction in this passage is likely based on events occurring in the Roman congregation—perhaps involving the Jewish believers' avoidance of certain foods in the face of the Gentile counterparts. How does Paul say that believers with these different dietary preferences should deal with their differences (see verses 1–4)?

_____

_____

_____

_____

_____

_____

6. Paul was aware that divisions in the church could tear apart a community. How does he say the believers are to view one another? What does he remind them about God's continual presence among their fellowship (see verses 5–12)?

_____

_____

_____

_____

_____

_____

The Law of Love (Romans 14:14–23)

14 I know and am convinced by the Lord Jesus that there is nothing unclean of itself; but to him who considers anything to be unclean, to him it is unclean. 15 Yet if your brother is grieved because of your food, you are no longer walking in love. Do not destroy with your food the one for whom Christ died. 16 Therefore do not let your good be spoken of as evil; 17 for the kingdom of God is not eating

and drinking, but righteousness and peace and joy in the Holy Spirit. [18] For he who serves Christ in these things is acceptable to God and approved by men.

[19] Therefore let us pursue the things which make for peace and the things by which one may edify another. [20] Do not destroy the work of God for the sake of food. All things indeed are pure, but it is evil for the man who eats with offense. [21] It is good neither to eat meat nor drink wine nor do anything by which your brother stumbles or is offended or is made weak. [22] Do you have faith? Have it to yourself before God. Happy is he who does not condemn himself in what he approves. [23] But he who doubts is condemned if he eats, because he does not eat from faith; for whatever is not from faith is sin.

---

7. Although the apostle Paul had been a former Pharisee steeped in Jewish traditions, he had come to the conclusion that "there is nothing unclean of itself." However, what caution does Paul add? How does this support his theme of unity in the church (see verses 14–18)?

_____

_____

_____

_____

8. Even though believers in Christ are now under "the law of liberty" and do not need to observe Jewish practices, what greater "law of love" should they follow (see verses 19–23)?

_____

_____

_____

_____

REVIEWING THE STORY

In this section of Romans, Paul outlined the believer's responsibility to human government. He pointed out that government authorities are appointed by God and, as such, believers should be subject to them. This includes paying taxes and fulfilling the typical duties of a citizen. Beyond honoring the government, believers also have a responsibility to follow Jesus' greatest command and honor one another by loving their neighbors as themselves. For Paul, loving one another means not judging one another—especially those who are deemed "weaker" in the church. Furthermore, Paul advised the believers to make sure their freedom in Christ did not cause others in the church to stumble. No one's actions should be a stumbling block to another.

9. According to Paul, what is the secret to being unafraid of authority (see Romans 13:3)?

10. Which five commandments does Paul say are summed up by the saying, "You shall love your neighbor as yourself" (see Romans 13:9)?

11. What overarching reason does Paul offer for why we should not judge one another (see Romans 14:12–13)?

12. What does Paul say about those who make sure they are not putting stumbling blocks in the way of other believers (see Romans 14:18)?

APPLYING THE MESSAGE

13. What should you do if you disagree with something that your government does?

14. What would be the proper response if a fellow Christian told you that something you do (or don't do) is a stumbling block to him or her?

REFLECTING ON THE MEANING

In this section of Romans, the apostle Paul states that he is "convinced by the Lord Jesus that there is nothing unclean of itself" (14:14). In particular, the believer in Christ is under no obligation to follow the Jewish practices found in the Old Testament law. However, Paul is quick to add three warnings on how believers should exercise this freedom. These warnings will likewise help us make sure we enjoy our freedom . . . but not at someone else's expense.

First, *we are not to let our freedom cause others to fall* (see verse 13). Christians who walk in love do not carelessly or purposely do things that cause others to fall into sin or to fall from grace into some legalistic trap. Sometimes, we can get so caught up in our rights as Christians that we flaunt them in front of other people—and we hurt them in the process. For years, C. H. Spurgeon, the great London preacher, saw nothing wrong with smoking a cigar. However, one day he walked past a store with a sign in the window that read, "The Cigar C. H. Spurgeon Smokes." From that day on, Spurgeon never again smoked a cigar, because he realized his freedom could cause another believer to stumble.

Second, *we are not to allow our freedom to cause others grief* (see verses 14–15). We are not acting in Christian love if we push our freedom in the faces of others. Anything we do that causes others to feel hurt violates the rule of love. But how do we know if something is a genuine hindrance or if the other person is trying to impose his or her ideas of what being a Christian means? The answer depends on whether the person is actually trying to grow spiritually or just sitting on the sidelines of the race and criticizing the runners. If the person is just a self-appointed judge, we are not obliged to cater to his or her feelings or conscience.

Third, *we are not to let our freedom cause God's work to be frustrated* (see verses 20–21). In this respect, Paul is talking about the work of God in another person: "We are His workmanship, created in Christ Jesus for good works" (Ephesians 2:10). God is at work in each of our lives. Paul was thus asking, "Are you going to destroy the work of God in somebody over some food? Why would you do that? We're called to pursue things that build others up and not get involved in things that tear others down."

Journaling Your Response

What are some ways you can encourage another believer through your choice *not* to do something—even though you have every right to do it?

THE EDIFICATION OF THE SAINTS

Romans 15:1–33

GETTING STARTED

What are some ways that you have been instructed by others in the faith?

SETTING THE STAGE

It is sad to see what happens when God's people forget they are one in Christ. The reality is that we are *not* all the same—a truth that Paul points out in this next section in his letter. We come from many different backgrounds and many different ideologies. However, we can all *learn* how to get along if we follow the principles found in the Word of God.

In the culture of the apostle Paul's day, there were many people in the churches who had grown up with a solid foundation of faith. They were godly Jewish converts who had not partaken in any of the Gentile pagan practices throughout the Roman Empire—or perhaps even been exposed to them. Now, these converts found themselves in communities with Gentiles from these backgrounds. To say the least, it was often difficult for these two groups to find common ground and get along with one another.

Yet Paul knew that it was essential for these groups to find unity if the community of believers was to survive. This is one of the reasons we find him calling for unity in his letters, extolling believers at odds with one another to try to understand the other party's viewpoint. In everything, Paul tries to help the members of the church learn how to support one another, with one member lifting up and strengthening another believer who is weak. As he writes:

> We then who are strong ought to bear with the scruples of the weak, and not to please ourselves. Let each of us please his neighbor for his good, leading to edification (Romans 15:1).

Paul's central message is there can be unity among believers when there is mutual acceptance and when individuals work toward the *edification* of one another. The key word is *edification*—one of Paul's favorite terms—which means to instruct another for the purpose of building him or her up in the faith. Those who believe they are strong in the faith should seek to *edify* those who may not be as strong. But above all, those who are strong should seek to bear the burdens of the weaker members and thus practice Jesus' command to love one another.

EXPLORING THE TEXT

Bearing One Others' Burdens (Romans 15:1–6)

---

¹ We then who are strong ought to bear with the scruples of the weak, and not to please ourselves. ² Let each of us please his neighbor for his good, leading to edification. ³ For even Christ did not please Himself; but as it is written, "The reproaches of those who reproached You fell on Me." ⁴ For whatever things were written before were written for our learning, that we through the patience and comfort of the Scriptures might have hope. ⁵ Now may the God of patience and comfort grant you to be like-minded toward one another, according to Christ Jesus, ⁶ that you may with one mind and one mouth glorify the God and Father of our Lord Jesus Christ.

---

1. Paul begins by addressing those who consider themselves "strong," as they have the greatest responsibility for putting his teachings into practice. What does he say should be our goal when it comes to our relationships with fellow believers (see verses 1–2)?

_____

_____

_____

_____

_____

_____

_____

_____

_____

2. For the first time in the letter, Paul holds up the example of Christ to his readers. How does Paul say they should imitate Him? What does it mean to be "like-minded toward one another" when it comes to supporting and edifying those in the church (see verses 4–6)?

_____

_____

_____

_____

_____

_____

_____

Glorify God Together (Romans 15:7–13)

⁷ Therefore receive one another, just as Christ also received us, to the glory of God. ⁸ Now I say that Jesus Christ has become a servant to the circumcision for the truth of God, to confirm the promises made to the fathers, ⁹ and that the Gentiles might glorify God for His mercy, as it is written:

> "For this reason I will confess to You among the Gentiles,
> And sing to Your name."

¹⁰ And again he says:

> "Rejoice, O Gentiles, with His people!"

¹¹ And again:

> "Praise the Lord, all you Gentiles!
> Laud Him, all you peoples!"

¹² And again, Isaiah says:

"There shall be a root of Jesse;
And He who shall rise to reign over the Gentiles,
In Him the Gentiles shall hope."

¹³ Now may the God of hope fill you with all joy and peace in believing, that you may abound in hope by the power of the Holy Spirit.

---

3. This passage contains Paul's directive to the believers based on what he has taught—to accept one another in love just as Jesus accepted them. How do the three passages he cites (from Psalm 18:9, Deuteronomy 32:43, and Psalm 117:1) reveal that God's plan was not just for the Jews? How does this relate to Paul's theme of unity (see Romans 15:7–11)?

_____

_____

_____

_____

_____

4. What does Paul say about the Gentiles in the prophecy he cites from Isaiah (see verse 12)?

_____

_____

_____

_____

_____

_____

The Minister to the Gentiles (Romans 15:14–21)

¹⁴ Now I myself am confident concerning you, my brethren, that you also are full of goodness, filled with all knowledge, able also to admonish one another. ¹⁵ Nevertheless, brethren, I have written more boldly to you on some points, as reminding you, because of the grace given to me by God, ¹⁶ that I might be a minister of Jesus Christ to the Gentiles, ministering the gospel of God, that the offering of the Gentiles might be acceptable, sanctified by the Holy Spirit. ¹⁷ Therefore I have reason to glory in Christ Jesus in the things which pertain to God. ¹⁸ For I will not dare to speak of any of those things which Christ has not accomplished through me, in word and deed, to make the Gentiles obedient—¹⁹ in mighty signs and wonders, by the power of the Spirit of God, so that from Jerusalem and round about to Illyricum I have fully preached the gospel of Christ. ²⁰ And so I have made it my aim to preach the gospel, not where Christ was named, lest I should build on another man's foundation, ²¹ but as it is written:

"To whom He was not announced, they shall see;
And those who have not heard shall understand."

5. Paul begins to conclude his letter by stating what he hopes his words will accomplish in the lives of the believers. What confidence does he express in how they will take his teachings? Why does he say that he wrote boldly on certain points (see verses 14–16)?

6. What things does Paul say he "will dare to speak of"? How does he describe his role and his overall aim for his ministry (see verses 18–21)?

_____

_____

_____

_____

_____

Plan to Visit Rome (Romans 15:22–33)

22 For this reason I also have been much hindered from coming to you. 23 But now no longer having a place in these parts, and having a great desire these many years to come to you, 24 whenever I journey to Spain, I shall come to you. For I hope to see you on my journey, and to be helped on my way there by you, if first I may enjoy your company for a while. 25 But now I am going to Jerusalem to minister to the saints. 26 For it pleased those from Macedonia and Achaia to make a certain contribution for the poor among the saints who are in Jerusalem. 27 It pleased them indeed, and they are their debtors. For if the Gentiles have been partakers of their spiritual things, their duty is also to minister to them in material things. 28 Therefore, when I have performed this and have sealed to them this fruit, I shall go by way of you to Spain. 29 But I know that when I come to you, I shall come in the fullness of the blessing of the gospel of Christ.

30 Now I beg you, brethren, through the Lord Jesus Christ, and through the love of the Spirit, that you strive together with me in prayers to God for me, 31 that I may be delivered from those in Judea who do not believe, and that my service for Jerusalem may be acceptable to the saints, 32 that I may come to you with joy by the will of God, and may be refreshed together with you. 33 Now the God of peace be with you all. Amen.

7. Paul opened the letter by stating he had planned to come to Rome but had been hindered from it (see 1:13). What reasons does he give in this passage for his delay? What does he envision as the benefits for himself and the community if they can meet (see 15:22–24)?

_____

_____

_____

_____

_____

8. What did the apostle Paul beg the Christians in Rome to do for him (see verses 30–32)?

_____

_____

_____

_____

_____

REVIEWING THE STORY

Paul began to wrap up his letter to the Romans with a series of exhortations. He encouraged the believers to embrace an active faith that manifested itself in their interactions with others. He stated those who are strong should help the weak—and that they should always look to please their neighbors instead of themselves. He lifted up Jesus as the supreme example of such behavior, challenging the church to accept one another just as Christ accepted them. Paul also shared the burden for his ministry and explained how he hoped his letter would be received. He again expressed his desire to visit the believers in Rome after he had finished delivering a contribution from the churches to the poor in Jerusalem. Finally, he pleaded for the Romans to pray for him as he continued his ministry as an apostle to the Gentiles.

9. How does Paul counter the popular viewpoints that "it's a dog-eat-dog world" and "only the strong survive" (see Romans 15:1)?

_____

_____

_____

_____

_____

10. In what manner does Paul say the believers should receive one another (see Romans 15:7)?

_____

_____

_____

_____

_____

11. Of what was Paul confident concerning the Roman believers (see Romans 15:14)?

_____

_____

_____

_____

_____

12. What was Paul's great desire concerning the Roman believers (see Romans 15:23–24)?

_____

_____

_____

_____

_____

_____

APPLYING THE MESSAGE

13. What is one thing you can do to help a believer who is weaker or less mature than you are?

_____

_____

_____

_____

_____

_____

14. To what "new" place in your own circle of influence can you take the gospel?

_____

_____

_____

_____

_____

_____

_____

REFLECTING ON THE MEANING

As the apostle Paul begins to conclude his letter to the believers in Rome, he asks them to join in his struggle by praying for him. Paul possessed a brilliant mind, an adventurous spirit, and a formidable reputation. Yet he was never too proud to ask others to pray for him!

It is interesting that almost none of the prayers Paul requested involved his health. Although he lived on the edge of danger and suffered great persecution, he rarely asked for physical protection. Instead, he almost always asked people to pray that he would be bold enough to speak the Word of God, that God would give him the words to say to people, that his messages would be Spirit-filled, and that lives would change when he preached.

There are three ways that Paul asked the believers in Rome to pray for him. First, he wanted to be prayed for *intentionally*. Generalities may have their place in prayer, but Paul sought targeted prayer for himself. His words remind us of the high priority he placed on prayer. "Now I beg you, brethren, through the Lord Jesus Christ, and through the love of the Spirit, that you strive together with me in prayers to God for me" (15:30).

Second, Paul wanted to be prayed for *intensely*. The word translated *strive* in verse 30 is the Greek word *agōnizo* (from which we get the word *agony*). Paul said, "I want you to *agonize* with me in prayer." He was reminding us that when we pray, we are joining together in a contest against the enemy. We are praying with the power of the Holy Spirit against the evil the enemy wants to do in our lives.

Third, Paul wanted to be prayed for *intelligently*. He wanted the Romans to be familiar with his situation so they would know how to pray. He asked them to pray for his safety in Jerusalem so he could fulfill his mission there. He asked them to pray that his mission would be met with success, for he was concerned the Jewish believers in need would reject such a generous offering from their wealthier non-Jewish counterparts. He also asked them to pray that God—if it was in His will—would make a way for him to come to visit them soon.

JOURNALING YOUR RESPONSE

What are some things that you need to pray for more intentionally, intensely, and intelligently?

GREETINGS AND WARNINGS

Romans 16:1–27

GETTING STARTED

What might Paul mention if he were writing to someone about your ministry for Christ?

_____

_____

_____

_____

_____

_____

_____

_____

_____

_____

_____

_____

_____

_____

_____

_____

_____

SETTING THE STAGE

The final chapter in Paul's letter to the believers in Rome is not one that we would necessarily recommend to a person who is new to the Christian faith. There are no less than thirty-five personal names mentioned in the chapter—people who are obscure to us today. We might be tempted to just skip over the chapter. However, by looking at these names, we gain insights into the heart of the apostle Paul. His words here comprise the most extensive and intimate expression of love that we find from the apostle.

Paul loved people with all his heart. He *remembered* their names and what they had done in service to God's kingdom. One of those was a woman named Phoebe (see 16:1–2). Paul begins by offering a letter of recommendation for her, which was a common practice in those days when a person moved from one place to another (see, for example, Acts 18:27). This practice was very important in the early days of the church, because people had no other means of communication. They carried these letters with them. In this case, Phoebe carried the letter from Corinth to Rome so that she would be well received there.

The name *Phoebe* is one of the names for the Roman goddess Diana. For that reason, many have concluded that Phoebe was a convert to Christianity out of the pagan culture of her day. When the early Christians became believers, they didn't always change their pagan names. So Phoebe kept her name, which means "bright and radiant." And when we read the commendation that Paul expressed about her, we discover that this was a fitting name.

Most of the other names in Paul's list do not appear anywhere else in the Bible. They are just common people serving—nothing extraordinary about them. Yet these "ordinary" Christians were just as important to Paul as Peter, James, and John were to Jesus and the early church. They serve as a reminder that we do not have to be "super" Christians in order to make a significant impact for the work God wants to do in our world. God can—and *will*—use anyone to achieve His purposes.

EXPLORING THE TEXT

Phoebe Is Commended (Romans 16:1–2)

¹ I commend to you Phoebe our sister, who is a servant of the church in Cenchrea, ² that you may receive her in the Lord in a manner worthy of the saints, and assist her in whatever business she has need of you; for indeed she has been a helper of many and of myself also.

1. Paul has just stated that he hoped to come to Rome but had been prevented from making the trip. Given this, it is likely that he entrusted this letter to Phoebe for delivery to the church. What does this say about Paul's faith in her (see verse 1)?

2. Why did Paul urge the Roman church to receive and assist Phoebe (see verse 2)?

Personal Greetings (Romans 16:3–16)

³ Greet Priscilla and Aquila, my fellow workers in Christ Jesus, ⁴ who risked their own necks for my life, to whom not only I give thanks,

but also all the churches of the Gentiles. ⁵ Likewise greet the church that is in their house.

Greet my beloved Epaenetus, who is the firstfruits of Achaia to Christ. ⁶ Greet Mary, who labored much for us. ⁷ Greet Andronicus and Junia, my countrymen and my fellow prisoners, who are of note among the apostles, who also were in Christ before me.

⁸ Greet Amplias, my beloved in the Lord. ⁹ Greet Urbanus, our fellow worker in Christ, and Stachys, my beloved. ¹⁰ Greet Apelles, approved in Christ. Greet those who are of the household of Aristobulus. ¹¹ Greet Herodion, my countryman. Greet those who are of the household of Narcissus who are in the Lord.

¹² Greet Tryphena and Tryphosa, who have labored in the Lord. Greet the beloved Persis, who labored much in the Lord. ¹³ Greet Rufus, chosen in the Lord, and his mother and mine. ¹⁴ Greet Asyncritus, Phlegon, Hermas, Patrobas, Hermes, and the brethren who are with them. ¹⁵ Greet Philologus and Julia, Nereus and his sister, and Olympas, and all the saints who are with them.

¹⁶ Greet one another with a holy kiss. The churches of Christ greet you.

---

3. While it may seem strange that Paul knew so many people in a church he had never visited, we have to remember the Emperor Claudius' edict had expelled the believers and caused them to travel to other places in the empire. We know this was true of Priscilla and Aquila, (see verses 3–5), whom Paul had met in the city of Corinth. Read Acts 18:1–4. What do you learn from these verses about their service and help to Paul?

4. The instruction to share a "holy kiss" served as a sign of the peace and love that Christ had brought among a divergent fellowship. Why is this instruction especially appropriate as Paul comes to the conclusion of his letter to the Roman believers?

_____

_____

_____

_____

A Final Warning (Romans 16:17–20)

17 Now I urge you, brethren, note those who cause divisions and offenses, contrary to the doctrine which you learned, and avoid them. 18 For those who are such do not serve our Lord Jesus Christ, but their own belly, and by smooth words and flattering speech deceive the hearts of the simple. 19 For your obedience has become known to all. Therefore I am glad on your behalf; but I want you to be wise in what is good, and simple concerning evil. 20 And the God of peace will crush Satan under your feet shortly.

The grace of our Lord Jesus Christ be with you. Amen.

5. Some scholars believe that Paul might have taken the pen from his scribe at this point and personally written this portion of the letter. Why do you think Paul felt compelled to interject this particular warning in between his greetings?

_____

_____

_____

_____

_____

6. What was Paul's specific warning to the believers? What did he say about the individuals that he mentions (see verses 17–18)?

_____

_____

_____

_____

Greetings from Paul's Friends (Romans 16:21–27)

²¹ Timothy, my fellow worker, and Lucius, Jason, and Sosipater, my countrymen, greet you.

²² I, Tertius, who wrote this epistle, greet you in the Lord.

²³ Gaius, my host and the host of the whole church, greets you. Erastus, the treasurer of the city, greets you, and Quartus, a brother. ²⁴ The grace of our Lord Jesus Christ be with you all. Amen.

²⁵ Now to Him who is able to establish you according to my gospel and the preaching of Jesus Christ, according to the revelation of the mystery kept secret since the world began ²⁶ but now made manifest, and by the prophetic Scriptures made known to all nations, according to the commandment of the everlasting God, for obedience to the faith—²⁷ to God, alone wise, be glory through Jesus Christ forever. Amen.

7. Paul did not accomplish his work for the gospel in isolation. In his letters, he frequently mentions coworkers who aided his efforts, most notably Timothy and Titus (see verse 21–24). What does his example say about how we should conduct our ministry for Christ?

_____

_____

_____

_____

8. The final verses represent Paul's *benediction* or *doxology* for the believers, which was a short prayer or blessing given at the end of a letter. What is the source of Paul's confidence as it relates to the believers in Rome (see verses 25–27)?

REVIEWING THE STORY

Paul concluded his letter with a series of greetings and requests. He offered a personal commendation for a servant named Phoebe and greetings to Priscilla and Aquila, his fellow Christian laborers and fellow tentmakers. He mentioned other believers who resided in Rome—people who had played crucial roles in his ministry. Paul ended with a final warning for the Romans to guard against dividers, deceivers, and false teachers in their midst. He added personal greetings from those who were with him in Corinth and then gave a closing benediction or doxology for the community.

9. What did Paul ask the Roman church to do in regard to Phoebe (see Romans 16:2)?

10. What did Priscilla and Aquila do that deserved special mention (see Romans 16:3–4)?

11. What do false teachers use to deceive the hearts of the simple (see Romans 16:18)?

12. With what words did Paul end his letter to the Romans (see Romans 16:27)?

APPLYING THE MESSAGE

13. If you singled out a few people who have made a difference in your spiritual life, whose names would you include? Why those individuals?

14. How can you recognize false teachers in the church today?

REFLECTING ON THE MEANING

As we reach the end of Paul's letter to the Romans, we come away with four final takeaways. The first is the *prominence of women in the early church*. Paul signals out Phoebe, Priscilla, Mary, Junia, Tryphena, Tryphosa, Persis, Rufus's mother, Julia, and Nereus's sister. These women served prominent roles in the church, and Paul recognized them as leaders. The number of women mentioned shows the honor placed on womanhood by Christianity. If you see a vibrant New Testament church today, you will find a church where women are carrying major responsibilities within the body and making an impact for Christ.

The second takeaway is the *priority of service in the early church*. Look at the people Paul mentioned. Priscilla and Aquila were "fellow workers in Christ Jesus" (verse 3). Mary "labored much" for Paul and his coworkers (verse 6). Urbanus was Paul's "fellow worker in Christ" (verse 9). Tryphena and Tryphosa "labored in the Lord" (verse 12). Persis "labored much in the Lord" (verse 12). This was a working church in Rome. These people did not just sit, soak, and sour. They got to work for God. We don't know what work these men and women did, but we know that it was important—so much so that Paul mentioned it.

The third takeaway is the *power of encouragement in the early church*. Paul models for us the affirmation and encouragement we all should demonstrate when we serve in a local assembly. Note how he mentions little things about each of these people to encourage them: Priscilla and Aquila risked their necks for him (see verses 3–4). Epaenetus was the beloved "firstfruits of Achaia to Christ" (verse 5). Andronicus and Junia were Paul's "countrymen . . . fellow prisoners," and "of note among the apostles" (verse 7). Stachys was "beloved" (verse 9). Apelles was "approved in Christ" (verse 10). Herodion was Paul's "countryman" (verse 11). Rufus was "chosen in the Lord" (verse 13). Each person had a place in Paul's heart.

The fourth takeaway is *unity in the early church*. What was it that held the Roman believers together? What was the glue in this church that was so special that Paul would write such a loving letter? It is evident from these few verses they were not all alike. They came from every walk of life, yet in their diversity, there was unity. Likewise, when Jesus Christ is the center of attraction in any church, there will be oneness, unity, and joy.

JOURNALING YOUR RESPONSE

What are ways you could encourage those who have helped you in your ministry for Christ?

LEADER'S GUIDE

Thank you for choosing to lead your group through this study from Dr. David Jeremiah on *The Letter of Romans*. Being a group leader has its own rewards, and it is our prayer that your walk with the Lord will deepen through this experience. During the twelve lessons in this study, you and your group will read selected passages from Romans, explore key themes in the letter based on teachings from Dr. Jeremiah, and review questions that will encourage group discussion. There are multiple components in this section that can help you structure your lessons and discussion time, so please be sure to read and consider each one.

BEFORE YOU BEGIN

Before your first meeting, make sure you and your group are well-versed with the content of the lesson. Group members should have their own copy of *The Letter of Romans* study guide prior to the first meeting so they can follow along and record their answers, thoughts, and insights. After the first week, you may wish to assign the study guide lesson as homework prior to the group meeting and then use the meeting time to discuss the content in the lesson.

To ensure everyone has a chance to participate in the discussion, the ideal size for a group is around eight to ten people. If there are more than ten people, break up the bigger group into smaller subgroups. Make sure the members are committed to participating each week, as this will help create stability and help you better prepare the structure of the meeting.

At the beginning of each week's study, start with the opening Getting Started question to introduce the topic you will be discussing. The members should answer briefly, as the goal is just for them to have an idea of the subject in their minds as you go over the lesson. This will allow the members to become engaged and ready to interact with the rest of the group.

After reviewing the lesson, try to initiate a free-flowing discussion. Invite group members to bring questions and insights they may have discovered to the next meeting, especially if they were unsure of the meaning of some parts of the lesson. Be prepared to discuss how biblical truth applies to the world we live in today.

WEEKLY PREPARATION

As the group leader, here are a few things that you can do to prepare for each meeting:

- *Be thoroughly familiar with the material in the lesson.* Make sure that you understand the content of each lesson so you know how to structure the group time and are prepared to lead the group discussion.

- *Decide, ahead of time, which questions you want to discuss.* Depending on how much time you have each week, you may not be able to reflect on every question. Select specific questions that you feel will evoke the best discussion.

- *Take prayer requests.* At the end of your discussion, take prayer requests from your group members and then pray for one another.

STRUCTURING THE DISCUSSION TIME

There are several ways to structure the duration of the study. You can choose to cover each lesson individually, for a total of twelve weeks of group meetings, or you can combine two lessons together per week, for a total of six weeks of group meetings. The following charts illustrate these options:

TWELVE-WEEK FORMAT

Week	Lessons Covered	Reading
1	Not Ashamed of the Gospel	Romans 1:1–32
2	The State of Humanity	Romans 2:1–3:31
3	Justification Through Faith	Romans 4:1–5:21
4	Spiritual Slavery	Romans 6:1–7:25
5	A Revolutionary Freedom	Romans 8:1–39
6	True and False Believers	Romans 9:1–33
7	God's Plan of Righteousness	Romans 10:1–21
8	The Destiny of Israel	Romans 11:1–36
9	Renewed Minds	Romans 12:1–21
10	Subject to Authority	Romans 13:1–14:23
11	The Edification of the Saints	Romans 15:1–33
12	Greetings and Warnings	Romans 16:1–27

SIX-WEEK FORMAT

Week	Lessons Covered	Reading
1	Not Ashamed of the Gospel / The State of Humanity	Romans 1:1–3:31
2	Justification Through Faith / Spiritual Slavery	Romans 4:1–7:25
3	A Revolutionary Freedom / True and False Believers	Romans 8:1–9:33
4	God's Plan of Righteousness / The Destiny of Israel	Romans 10:1–11:36
5	Renewed Minds / Subject to Authority	Romans 12:1–14:23
6	The Edification of the Saints / Greetings and Warnings	Romans 15:1–16:27

In regard to organizing your time when planning your group Bible study, the following two schedules, for sixty minutes and ninety minutes, can give you a structure for the lesson:

Section	60 Minutes	90 Minutes
Welcome: Members arrive and get settled	5 minutes	10 minutes
Getting Started Question: Prepares the group for interacting with one another	10 minutes	10 minutes
Message: Review the lesson	15 minutes	25 minutes
Discussion: Discuss questions in the lesson	25 minutes	35 minutes
Review and Prayer: Review the key points of the lesson and have a closing time of prayer	5 minutes	10 minutes

As the group leader, it is up to you to keep track of the time and keep things moving according to your schedule. If your group is having a good discussion, don't feel the need to stop and move on to the next question. Remember, the purpose is to pull together ideas and share unique insights on the lesson. Encourage everyone to participate, but don't be concerned if certain group members are more quiet. They may just be internally reflecting on the questions and need time to process their ideas before they can share them.

GROUP DYNAMICS

Leading a group study can be a rewarding experience for you and your group members—but that doesn't mean there won't be challenges. Certain members may feel uncomfortable discussing topics that they consider very personal and might be afraid of being called on. Some members might have disagreements on specific issues. To help prevent these scenarios, consider the following ground rules:

- If someone has a question that may seem off topic, suggest that it be discussed at another time, or ask the group if they are okay with addressing that topic.

- If someone asks a question you don't know the answer to, confess that you don't know and move on. If you feel comfortable, invite other group members to give their opinions or share their comments based on personal experience.
- If you feel like a couple of people are talking much more than others, direct questions to people who may not have shared yet. You could even ask the more dominating members to help draw out the quiet ones.
- When there is a disagreement, encourage the group members to process the matter in love. Invite members from opposing sides to evaluate their opinions and consider the ideas of the other members. Lead the group through Scripture that addresses the topic, and look for common ground.

When issues arise, encourage your group to think of Scripture: "Love one another" (John 13:34), "If it is possible, as much as it depends on you, live peaceably with all men" (Romans 12:18), and, "Be swift to hear, slow to speak, slow to wrath" (James 1:19).

ABOUT
Dr. David Jeremiah and Turning Point

Dr. David Jeremiah is the founder of Turning Point, a ministry committed to providing Christians with sound Bible teaching relevant to today's changing times through radio and television broadcasts, audio series, books, and live events. Dr. Jeremiah's teaching on topics such as family, prayer, worship, angels, and biblical prophecy forms the foundation of Turning Point.

David and his wife, Donna, reside in El Cajon, California, where he serves as the senior pastor of Shadow Mountain Community Church. David and Donna have four children and twelve grandchildren.

In 1982, Dr. Jeremiah brought the same solid teaching to San Diego television that he shares weekly with his congregation. Shortly thereafter, Turning Point expanded its ministry to radio. Dr. Jeremiah's inspiring messages can now be heard worldwide on radio, television, and the internet.

Because Dr. Jeremiah desires to know his listening audience, he travels nationwide holding ministry rallies and spiritual enrichment conferences that touch the hearts and lives of many people. According to Dr. Jeremiah, "At some point in time, everyone reaches a turning point; and for every person, that moment is unique, an experience to hold onto forever. There's so much changing in today's world that sometimes it's difficult to choose the right path. Turning Point offers people an understanding of God's Word and seeks to make a difference in their lives."

Dr. Jeremiah has authored numerous books, including *Escape the Coming Night* (Revelation), *The Handwriting on the Wall* (Daniel), *Overcoming Loneliness, Prayer—The Great Adventure, God in You* (Holy Spirit), *When*

Your World Falls Apart, Slaying the Giants in Your Life, My Heart's Desire, Hope for Today, Captured by Grace, Signs of Life, What in the World Is Going On?, The Coming Economic Armageddon, I Never Thought I'd See the Day!, God Loves You: He Always Has—He Always Will, Agents of the Apocalypse, Agents of Babylon, Revealing the Mysteries of Heaven, People Are Asking . . . Is This the End?, A Life Beyond Amazing, Overcomer, and *The Book of Signs.*

STAY CONNECTED
to Dr. David Jeremiah

Take advantage of two great ways to let Dr. David Jeremiah give you spiritual direction every day!

Turning Points **Magazine and Devotional**

Receive Dr. David Jeremiah's magazine, *Turning Points*, each month and discover:

- Thematic study focus
- 48 pages of life-changing reading
- Relevant articles
- Special features
- Daily devotional readings
- Bible study resource offers
- Live event schedule
- Radio & television information

Request *Turning Points* magazine today!

(800) 947-1993
www.DavidJeremiah.org/Magazine

Daily Turning Point E-Devotional

Start your day off right! Find words of inspiration and spiritual motivation waiting for you on your computer every morning! Receive a daily e-devotion communication from David Jeremiah that will strengthen your walk with God and encourage you to live the authentic Christian life.

Request your free e-devotional today!

(800) 947-1993
www.DavidJeremiah.org/Devo

New Bible Study Series
from Dr. David Jeremiah

The Jeremiah Bible Study Series captures Dr. David Jeremiah's
forty-plus years of commitment to teaching the whole Word of God.
Each volume contains twelve lessons for individuals and groups to
explore what the Bible says, what it meant to the people at the time it
was written, and what it means to us today. Out of his lifelong ministry
of *delivering the unchanging Word of God to an ever-changing world*,
Dr. Jeremiah has written this Bible-strong study series focused not on
causes, current events, or politics, but on the solid truth of Scripture.

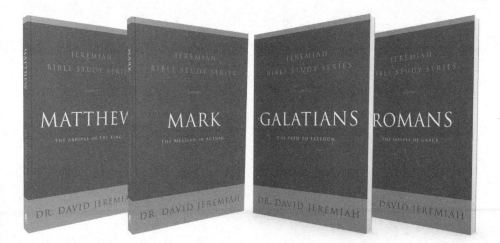

9780310091493	Matthew	9780310091554	John	9780310091646	1 Corinthians
9780310091516	Mark	9780310091608	Acts	9780310097488	2 Corinthians
9780310091530	Luke	9780310091622	Romans	9780310091660	Galatians

Available now at your favorite bookstore.
More volumes coming soon.

THOMAS NELSON
Since 1798